In dedication of all the wonderful and beautiful inspiring souls who have been the source of inspiration to the world…

THERE IS ALWAYS A DOOR...

There	It is not here, but somewhere "there" signifying I have to make an effort, take actions to reach from where I am to where I want to be, what I want to become.
is	It is in the present tense, that is in the "now" nothing to do with the past nor the future.
always	It exists at all times; I only need to tune in.
a	It is that very fraction of moment, that opening, that one opportunity which I need to seize.
door	It is what leads me to newer possibilities, newer horizons, since in life, I don't arrive, I keep arriving.
...	A single dot is a period, a full stop which marks an end, but when two more dots are added, it signifies continuity, and life is nothing but a continuum.

Girish Agrawal

INDIA • SINGAPORE • MALAYSIA

ISBN 979-8-89186-837-3

Contents

Foreword

I have a vivid memory of my first meeting with Girish Agrawal. I had joined the school in the middle of the term during Class VII and understood on the first day that "Hand-ball Cricket" was a popular game among the students. I wanted to play too, so I had to approach Girish. I found him in the corner of the garden, immersed in making a ball out of waste newspapers and rubber bands. Little did I know then that a super-strong friendship was about to blossom, and along the beautiful way I would be privy to some extraordinary inspiration-filled moments. Moments that would make me wonder time and again as to how Girish makes it happen **in spite of...**

Girish has worked hard to cultivate exceptional mental strength, unwavering commitment to what is once decided, fluid execution skills, and a sense of surrender.

Despite repeated setbacks, he bounces back due to his mental strength, be it a spine-breaking accident, long-distance cycling, or marathon running. I have been a witness to his commitment to excelling in football during his youth, being Leo Club President in his mid-twenties, and studying law in his mid-forties, to name a few. Effortless execution of tasks at hand, be it CA studies in Mumbai, handling finance functions in an MNC corporate, or organizing events.

What I value the most is his ability to surrender. After all that he could possibly do, he was at peace in each episode, whether life-threatening surgery of the spine, a decision to turn to alternate medicine for a difficult-to-handle medical complication, or a long delay in his appointment as a Tribunal member (ITAT). Each had an element of surrender to the infinite universal intelligence.

A man is known by his deeds. Through this book, Girish has been very kind in sharing his experiences. Each experience is accompanied by his thoughts, constraints, circumstances, options, decisions, and actions. Apart from being written in simple language, he has chosen to describe experiences that are relevant and insightful. They strike a chord and leave the reader with the utmost positivity and hope.

With his unique combination of mental strength, commitment, execution, and surrender, he has deciphered the code of living a wholesome life in his own experiential way. For those who are looking to crack the code of their lives, this book can turn out to be the door. **Yes, There Is Always A Door...**

Himaanshu Kansal

Laughed and cried with Girish

My Gratitude...

First and foremost, to '*my Master*', my beloved *Mahatria*, my source of faith and strength.

My persona is like that of the moon, which does not have any light of its own. Everything is of the sun, 'the source of source'. There is a 'factor of dependency' as the moon receives light from the sun and reflects it very differently. The same light has different manifestations, by the sun and by the moon, serving the purpose differently. Similarly, nothing of my own. All these expressions are nothing but the reflection of the learnings and experiences of Your teachings, nothing of me, and everything of You. Mahatria for me is my internal, self-talking language by which I think, I talk, I breathe, and I live every moment of this life. My reverential gratitude for being there, carrying me like a 'baby monkey'...

गुरू गोविन्द दोऊ खड़े, काके लागूं पांय।

बलिहारी गुरू अपने गोविन्द दियो बताय।।

संत कबीर कह गये,

गुरु ने ही गोविन्द से हमारा परिचय कराया है इसलिए गुरु का स्थान गोविन्द से भी ऊँचा है।

To '*my Lord Krishn*', an epitome of evolved consciousness in an embodied form, a complete incarnation, multidimensional, manifestation of unconditional love, exuberance of joy, compassion, detached engagement, beauty, celebrations, situational brilliance, devotion, energy and enthusiasm, intensity, empathy, justice, equanimity, poise and composure, benevolence and the list goes endless. *Krishn* consciousness reverberates and intrinsically resonates with my life journey lived so far with all its complexities. All my endeavors are to create as many *Krishn* moments as I can, dancing with life and with death, to embrace the consciousness. Oh, my lord, let this expression through me also be the reflection of moments of *Krishn's* expression. *Thy will prevails…*

To '*my source for the power of words*', two of my loving English teachers, namely respected Abha Ma'am and Veena Roy Ma'am who taught me the nuances of the language and allowed me to play with it to create beautiful expressions. I cherish and find myself equally comfortable with the Hindi language, and for its smooth flow through me, I owe it all first to my mother, who also has a flair for writing. I also owe it equally to my loving Hindi teachers, namely respected Mutha Ma'am, Shandilya Ma'am, and Kalia Ma'am. My reverential gratitude to all of them for holding my hand and not giving up on me, and most importantly, for carrying me in their hearts, even in the present time after more than thirty years of passing out from the school.

To my loving grandfather in his loving remembrance, whom I fondly cherish in my memories as '*मेरे बाबा*' who gave me the divine attributes of unconditional love and care. I feel your presence all around.

To my darling son, '*मेरा बच्चन सिंग*' Akshat for giving me the feeling of godliness. Creation is through the Creator. Parenting Akshat and seeing him grow through my spouse Arpita, and me is leading to a beautiful creation. His sharing of maturity with a childlike expression coupled with contemporary perspectives has always opened new dimensions of my understanding of various aspects of my life, ever since he arrived in our lives. I was amazed at his comprehension of the first draft of all this writing and the feedback to make course corrections that have been incorporated in the one in your hand. Even otherwise, he is an intrinsic part of my journey, and I could not have taken up this expression of words without him. He is my underlying source of confidence and assurance for letting me be myself.

To '*my boon companions*', Himaanshu and Atul, for all the growing and learning we have been experiencing together, whether in our close physical proximity or being in faraway geographies. The chemistry of this beautiful 'trilogy' is beyond any judgments or expectations. Blessed are those who have at least one relationship where one can get psychologically naked, and I have two such confidants. This relationship is a mirror reflecting on me. There are no explanations or justifications for anything done or not done. It's the space where my being gains relevance. The process of life has worked on us and with us, giving us humongous exposures and experiences that culminate in this piece of expression with colors filled by you.

With the 'lighthouse' in every facet of my life, I did my part to the best of my ability, and the rest has been history so far, arriving where I am today. In this domain of expressing myself through my word power, Megha Bajaj is '*my lighthouse*'. I could sail in the deep waters and anchor to her wherever and whenever the need arose while creating this book. Thank you for being the 'lighthouse' and allowing me to get anchored.

To N. Raju and Vishnupriya Raju, '*my connect*' for the breakthrough moments that have led to the synchronicities of me meeting Megha Bajaj to unfold this facet of my persona of expressing through the 'Wonders of Words (WoW)'. All this transpired when Raju and I, along with Vishnupriya and Akshat, sat on the floor in a hotel in Chennai in April 2023. I spoke to Raju about Megha and WoW, which I had explored on the website. In that moment, that very special moment, a trigger occurred that spoke to me somewhere deep inside that I needed to leverage 'my word power' for the larger benefits. And here I am, for all the good to happen through the connections...

There are several traits for which I can associate myself with several *'best-in-class'* personalities, including my teachers, coaches, friends, colleagues, and associates. I am much more than a biological product. I am the sum total of life experientially lived so far. A big thanks to all of them for bringing exclamation marks into my life.

Why This Book?

Deep inside somewhere, there had been triggers that had been yelling at me that I needed to leverage 'my word power', which nature has bestowed upon me, for the larger benefits. Expressing myself through words in the written form has always given me a better sense of completeness and satisfaction in the communication of my thoughts, feelings, and emotions.

Life has been extremely rewarding in all dimensions of life ever since childhood. It has been so *'in spite of...'* while experiencing three major near-death experiences (NDEs). I cherish every moment I have lived so far, reaching where I have reached as of now. There is a plethora of success stories from various facets of my personality, be it academics, sports, leadership roles, social welfare events, public events, professional pursuits, adventures, creativity and innovations, and so on.

"Fifty is the new zero," my Master says.

As I complete fifty revolutions around the sun on December 29th, 2023, and start afresh, I present to the world this book on my life lived so far to motivate you to go that far, and even beyond. With such an intense life of experiential living, it is impossible to capture everything in just one book, which also happens to be my maiden attempt. This first step has given me immense motivation to go as far as I can in expressing myself through the power of words, which I shall keep sharing at appropriate times in the future.

I share my life story lived so far by talking about my school days, my upbringing, developing my career path, climbing the ladder of success on various dimensions, having a deeply rooted spiritual connection of faith and surrender, getting from the world by giving and flowing with the flow like a river, to ultimately submerge in the vast ocean, for the eternal unison. These stories and experiences only reflect my sincere attempts to actualize and maximize the potential bestowed upon me.

I am a library of experiences. These experiences are making me aware of the mechanics that shape my destiny. They give me a pleasant sensation of knowing. Experiential living has made me trust my intuition and allow the flow to flow. It allows me to focus on what is working right for me, making life feel good. Reading from these experiences gives me the ability to shift my focus to where I want to give my attention and where I want to place my awareness. They allow me to accept my worthiness, my differences, my individuality, and my uniqueness.

Living with struggle and having challenges in life are two different things. There is no struggle either in life or in nature, but only striving. Challenges lead to striving, which in turn makes me grow, discover, and evolve. I am an evolving consciousness.

I write and express all of this only to inspire, and not to create any impression upon you or to convince you of the learnings that I have gained from my own personal experiences.

Each one has to tread one's own path, walk that far to arrive there, and then again walk further. In your own walking, these expressions of mine may act as catalysts to trigger certain sparks within you for igniting the fire and enable you to absorb the light and warmth therefrom.

I am unique, the only one so far, and there won't be anyone else like me in the future either. The same is the case with even you. This being the absolute truth, these expressions of writing need not be taken as a checklist to replicate with my experiences and learnings of life.

01

In Spite Of…

In our home or workplace, when a power failure occurs and darkness surrounds us, in that instant fraction of a moment, our mind automatically looks for a source of light, be it a mobile handset torch, candle, etc. It is an opportunity to adopt a solution-centric approach for some while a problem for others.

In that very moment of the collision of the front left side of our taxi with the rear right side of the truck ahead of us in the wee hours around 3:30 a.m. on November 8th, 2014, while returning from Nagpur to Indore via Bhopal after dropping my cousin there, my mind looked out for a solution to address the traumatic situation, my approach being eternally optimistic.

A grave road accident was met by us, approximately 80 kilometers away from Indore while traveling with my spouse Arpita, who was sitting on the back seat and our close to twelve-year-old son Akshat, who was sleeping on her lap, while I was sitting on the front left seat with a seat belt on and the driver driving the car.

In that fraction of a moment (*only a fraction*), my eyes closed, but the real eyes got fixated on that flash of amber I experienced in the moment of the collision (I would rather call it the moment of '*unison*'). I experienced the light flowing in, lighting up the deep space inside and outside. A surge of powerful energy, which can't be seen, was deeply experienced.

The *unison* occurred of the life energy, of the body and mind as the radiant light, soaked in.

Synchronicities flowed-in miraculously to take control of the situation as if everything was already orchestrated with rehearsals done in advance.

I was wearing the seat belt, which I always do. After that moment of the collision, Arpita and Akshat being in a much safer condition compared to mine, called for help from around, '108' ambulance had arrived, people were breaking open the front door of the car to take me out, and I asked with clarity to give support to my neck and a collar was available in the ambulance (though seldom found otherwise), first aid was given.

I was drowsy but alive with sensory perceptions and an active brain. On the way to Indore, I was guiding Arpita to make phone calls to doctors to arrange the emergency medical aid at the right hospital when we arrive in Indore.

I asked her to type the names I said on my mobile, to make calls and update them about the exigency. I spelled '*B I N D*' and the first connect was with Dr. Bindal who was on vacation in Kerala, then I spelled '*A S H I*' which connected to Mr. Ashiq, a client at Dewas (40 kilometers from Indore) for on-route support and then Himaanshu, my childhood buddy. For the intrinsic bond I share with him, referring to him as a 'childhood buddy' is too little to express what he means to me. A call was also made by her to my younger sister Chanchal and my parents.

On the way, while lying in the ambulance in bear minimum blood-stained undergarments on a cold morning of early November with fresh bleeding wounds and pieces of broken windshield of the car all over the upper body, I kept telling the driver to maintain an easy pace, avoiding jerks and not to rush. While lying down, intermittently, I could see the blue sky from the side window of the ambulance, which gave me a *sense of connection* with the enormous vastness that spread all around me, taking care of me and my family.

Himaanshu and Apurva had arrived at Dewas, driving down from Indore in the wee hours of the day on our call. Apurva is yet another vital link in this chain of life synchronicities. My stretcher had locked up in the ambulance when medical staff at a hospital in Dewas tried to get me out. I was guided internally that if I was moved by the hospital staff even by an inch, everything would collapse, hence that *'locking up'* of the stretcher was by the Almighty. Later, I was told that this hospital had nothing to make my condition better than what prevailed at that moment. Hence, there was no point in moving me out of the ambulance. Locking up of my stretcher, therefore, had a valid reason.

At the same moment, miraculously, I sat up in a single move with a jerk for a bout of vomit in front of Himaanshu. I had *'an eye connect'* with him, exchanged the *'assurance'* and laid back gently. It was a perfect abs crunch with my collared neck in an absolutely still and neutral position.

Friends and teachers have been the driving force for the journey of this life and have played a vital role in shaping me. We will talk more about this in the later chapters to come.

We arrived at the hospital lined up through Siddharth (Sid), my schoolmate. One of the best-known neurosurgeons in the city was associated with this hospital. At the emergency entrance gate, they took over. From here on, I went into a coma-like condition, losing my sensory connection to the physicality of everything around me. I distinctly remember, after this point, I was no longer active, the way I was while traveling in the ambulance.

There was acute damage to my C5 and C6 vertebrae in the spine column at the neck region apart from several other wounds and injuries. The right collarbone was broken, the center and forehead were torn, and both hands were severely wounded. The doctor had sounded the uncertainties about the quality of life, post-surgery of my spine.

It is a duration of almost sixty hours from that fraction of the moment of collision to the successful completion of my surgery of the spine which has become a *'point of reference'* for the rest of my life. What transpired in these sixty hours is incredible – chaos for the world *'outside'* of me but absolute bliss, sacred and divine *'inside'*. In fact, compartmentalizing into outside and inside is not appropriate, but I am not able to find any other words to give a perspective. Truly, it's all one, the whole. It led to remembrances, retrievals, and explorations of what lay within, *'soul-knowing'* experiences.

For these sacred sixty hours, let's begin from the beginning...

In that splash of flash, I could listen to the quietness, feel the stillness. Deep space in the Universe is filled with light; darkness is all lit up by the stars. The same was the experience with my eyes closed.

There was no sense of time. Nothing like day or night. It was all in one plane, all in the state of stillness. There was nothing to distinguish between my past, what I was experiencing in the present, and my imagination of the future. All existed at one instance. Let me try and explain this with a visualization, though extremely difficult to put all that experience into words –

There are rail tracks that are laid down and are fixated to the ground. There are several trains that run from one point to another in their own schedule of arrival and departure. Their movement is monitored and requires discipline as they run on the same rail track, which is available equally to all the trains, coming and going. Now, consider the rail track as the 'time' and trains as the individual life, each one is. Visualize time being constant, fixated to the ground, all of it available to each life in every single instance whether starting from here or from anywhere on the rail track. All of the rail track is available to each one, wherever that one is.

I experienced the time element as a stationary rail track, all of it available to me, always. It has always been there and will continue to be so. I could move in any direction as I chose and lead the life to reach where I want to be. I was on the track, in the present, and we all know, a present is always beautiful since the present is also called a 'gift'.

I was neither frustrated nor there were any worries. Everything was in plenty. I was seeing the bigger picture to realize that things appeared in their own time, according to their rhythm and synchronicities. There was nothing I could do to control them. I was able to see and feel that in the grand scheme of things, everything is perfect.

My focus was on all that was going right, in the present, on the blessings. The invisible source of energy had all the control, facilitating the minutest support, resource, or thing for taking care of everything required. From the moment of collision or *unison*, as I call it, all my actions and thoughts were guided by the energy to take care of my badly injured body and my family members who accompanied me. My mind was active by itself. No force was required to make it work.

All were in harmony as thoughts, words, and actions, all of them were in sync.

I knew trying to do anything from my side would obstruct or halt the flow and slow down the entire process. I avoided getting in the way of the flow and preferred just to be with it. The patience was impeccable. I just needed to wait, and everything took care of itself.

The only feeling I could feel was of completeness, though at the bodily level, there was so much that was broken, so many injuries, several wounds, glass pieces pierced all over, the entire body inflamed, swollen, and torn. In spite of all this, I was at an extremely deep relaxation point inside. There was no stress but bliss. I was wondering why others around me were not able to feel the same bliss. I knew they had to just let go to feel what I was feeling and experiencing.

There is no struggle in nature. There are so many activities in our own body for which we have to do nothing. It is taken care of on its own. The flow of blood, beating of the heart, growth of cells or nails, digestion of food, and so on.

I was alert and acted on the inspired ideas flowing in my mind. The only thing required was to 'stay connected'. It was a connection with the higher realms of consciousness. The choice I made at that moment of choosing the frequency of higher and positive vibrations made all the difference. I have always carried a solution-centric and eternally optimistic approach to life which has made it happen. Generally, we tend to tune in with the negative frequencies of doubt, disbelief, or disappointment, which I never opt for.

It is like choosing a radio frequency to tune in to play the music one wants to listen to. All the radio frequencies are there in the air, but the choice depends on us. Choosing the right frequency is a matter of choice and not chance. Choosing it right gives the desired music. I have to find my way to tune in with the desired frequency to get the music I want. The same applies to the fulfillment of desires I create.

I distinctly recall and remember the room in the first hospital I was put up in immediately upon our arrival at Indore, along with heavy traction to keep my spine in the right position, my bed being in one corner. The door opened in front on the diagonally opposite corner.

I could listen to the conversation between my mother and my younger sister outside of the room, they being very concerned since my father and all others were in indecisive mode for the next course of action with my state of affairs. I had the visualization and sense of stressed and agitated conversations taking place for the uncertainties that prevailed about my life.

However, for me, it was as if I had reached the most relaxed state possible. I could feel the freshness. I felt the strength, the light, and the calmness. Everything looked clear and clean, inviting. I was feeling and enjoying the feeling. I allowed and opened myself to receive the abundance.

I was where I always wanted to be, to see my own beautiful reflection. The myths I had grown up with were all broken and shattered. There were no questions, as all the misunderstandings instilled were cleared.

My fears had vanished. What people thought was of no concern to me. Their opinion did not matter to me. It was my life, and it mattered the most to me. Whatever was happening was just right, and I had to be in the flow; no other technique would work for me except for being in the present and going with the flow. I had to only allow the energy to flow through me; there was nothing right or wrong.

One of my friends, Dr. Sangram, who is a pediatric surgeon, arrived sometime in the day as a *'divine intervention'*. Standing toward my legs on the side of the bed, he said,

"*Girish, kaise ho?*" [Girish, how are you?]

I said, "*Behtar hun.*" [Much better.]

He asked, "*Do you know who is operating on you?*"

I replied, "No."

He continued, "*Don't you think the best surgeon should operate on you?*"

I asked, "*Who is that?*"

He replied, "*You should find out.*"

I asked him to give me some options. He gave three names as options from whom I needed to find out who was the best for me to operate up on. He suggested three names, which also included a team of two doctors. He then left the room.

I was totally uninformed about the indecisiveness and the chaos going on, as well as about the traumatic injuries I had sustained. Various scans were done all over my body after our arrival, from which they diagnosed my grave condition. For me, my understanding was based on my internal sense, which was guiding me through.

I called Himaanshu to assist me with the task given by Dr. Sangram.

I told him with absolute clarity, *"Call Sonu Da and tell him the three names. Ask him who is the best among them, and on hearing the first name, disconnect the phone."*

Himaanshu left the room, and I assumed that he would come back with the result. Later, Dr. Sangram came in the evening. Again, this sense of time of the day to me was not by looking at the clock or by seeing through the window but was internally guided.

Again, standing on the legs side of my bed, he asked,

"Girish, pataa kiya, doctor kaa, unn teen naamon mein se?" [Did you find a doctor out of the three names?]

I was jolted by this question since I was reminded that Himaanshu had not turned up with this piece of information. I asked to call him immediately. He came rushing into the room. At that moment, he got a nasty blast from me for missing such a vital thing. Standing on my left-hand side, he made a call to Sonu *Da* and asked him about the three names. On hearing the first name, he told me that it was the team of two doctors and disconnected the phone call.

On this piece of information, I then asked Dr. Sangram how that team of the two doctors was, as surgeons and as individuals.

He said, *"They have excellent hands as surgeons, and as individuals, they are very good human beings."*

I counter-questioned him, *"How do you know them?"*

He answered, *"We have worked together at a hospital for quite some time, and I know them personally; they are very good friends of mine."*

The decision was taken immediately, and I instructed Himaanshu to ensure that only they operated on me.

Most importantly, I was told that this team of two doctors worked at a different hospital, and at that time, we were at the first hospital where we initially arrived. According to the doctor there, shifting me was life-threatening and would be fatal. In absolute, clear, and authoritative terms, I again instructed to shift me to that hospital where the team of the two doctors worked. It took quite an effort by my caretakers to get clearance for the shifting process.

All these conversations and interfaces were validated much later, when my life returned to normalcy. Everybody believed that they were talking to the person, Girish, who was lying on the bed. They all missed the vital fact that Girish was in a coma-like condition with high levels of sedatives, painkillers, and several lifesaving drugs injected into the body and had lost sensory perceptions of the physicality around him.

I know who I was during those interactions and from where I was conversing with people around me. I and my body were two different entities. I was not willing to go, and my body was not good enough to take me in. It was a game of willpower, which life threw me in, and I had to win as I told myself, I couldn't go, for so much had to be done yet...

Even today, Himaanshu doesn't miss any opportunity to pinch me for the nasty blast he got in those moments. At the same time, he doesn't fail to appreciate the clear-headedness with which the entire communication took place [me using the authoritative words '*I instructed*'].

In all this, I had been in the now, which was the true moment and the point of my power. In that moment, I knew, I was aware, and I could observe myself, my thoughts, and everything. I was the observer of me. Each such moment was the moment of experiencing consciousness.

Like everyone else, I have also grown up into a complex being out of my thoughts, ideas, dreams, and desires. As an observer, I know that some part of me knows this. However, I don't know how I know this. I am a part of life like a wave is part of the ocean. I can't exist outside of the Universe, just as a wave can't exist outside of the ocean. I don't have to understand everything with my conscious and logical mind.

During that moment, my subconscious organized itself to clear out the unhelpful ideas and thoughts that were not beneficial for my wellbeing. I was being pulled to that side, but I was not giving up, with my body lying on the bed in its broken form, not capable enough to be in it. I was clear with my choice, *'to be with life'*.

Life is a mysterious energy that nobody knows from where it comes. But it is there; it is real. That energy always exists, though it keeps changing its form. I am that energy too and have changed my form several times, including in the present life since my birth. One form affects the other, for sure. My childhood affected my adolescent period, which in turn had an impact on my youth, and it continues in the same manner, moving ahead as of now.

I had set my intentions very clearly to come back since there was so much to do, so much to add to life, so much to contribute to the world around me, and so much to expand my horizons. I knew I was not separate from the creative force and was being taken care of with the utmost trust to live happily ever after. That divine intervention I narrated took place to set my body right and make it capable of assisting me in serving the purpose of life.

It was like being in the mother's womb, where everything is taken care of in all respects. I had food, oxygen, nourishment, temperature, care, sleep, everything. Assurance prevailed that nature takes care of everything; I didn't have to worry or interfere in its process, trusting that it knew all the details. There was no need to check-up on the fulfilment of my desires. I just needed to let go, be aware of what was working well, and be grateful, expressing gratitude. Trying to do anything would interfere with the processes of nature.

Whatever the desire, there is a way for it to be achieved. The only thing required is to set the intentions for it, which I did.

In short, it's all about
letting go...
trusting the Universe...
and being grateful...

The images and impressions also got cleared, which were no longer needed for the journey of life ahead. I was safe. I was wondering without any wandering of my mind. I could see so many beautiful images to visualize the amazing life which I could live in the times to come. It also brought before me some nostalgic pictures from the past that have caused deep positive impressions on me.

The next day at the hospital where I had been shifted, in the afternoon, in the aisle of the floor where the Operation Theater (OT) was, all gathered to see me off for the successful procedure. For them, uncertainties still prevailed. It was around 2:30 p.m., and while crossing the aisle, by pulling my eyes way up and backward, I connected with Akshat, standing with all of them. With my stretcher slowly moving ahead, I spoke in a loud and clear voice, telling him with cent-percent conviction and assurance,

"Akshat, don't worry, I will come back. That's my promise, and you know Papa keeps his promise."

I saw his face with a waving hand, and my eyes slowly closed down with the stretcher moving into the holding area outside of the OT. There was a reciprocation which I felt in his eyes.

I happened to visit this area after almost six months of my surgery for a regular check-up, as doctors had called me in the OT zone. When I went there, I could relate to the place so distinctly and recall where my stretcher was resting, from where all the hustle and bustle was coming up, where the entry door was, and so many other small things. It was a known area for me.

In the OT, the medical staff had shifted my body on the OT table. Beaming lights were on. My head was rested carefully. One, Dr. Iyengar was exactly behind my center head, and the other, Dr. Newalkar was on the right side of the first one. At that point in time, I never knew who was who, as I had never met them. I could relate to all these details later.

The doctor who was on the right side yelled at me,

"Abe saale, tu hai kaun? Subah se tere liye pachhis phone aa chuke hain ki mera khaas hai dhyan rakhna, mera bhai hai, sambhal lena, vagairah vagairah… pareshan kar diya tere phones ne." [Who the hell are you? Since morning, I have received several phone calls to take good care of you.]

I replied with calm and composure,

"Doctor, don't worry. I am in the hands of God. Please go ahead; everything will be alright."

I surrendered…

Now that I knew what was inside, I realized it was time to come outside; almost sixty hours had elapsed. With my surgery over, for which I didn't know what was done by the doctors, I had the assurance deep within that my body was now capable of allowing me to lead the life I wanted to live. It was time to come back, as I promised Akshat on the afternoon of November 10th, 2014, in the aisle, while I was taken to the Operation Theater on the stretcher. And I did.

Himaanshu celebrates his birthday on November 10th, and I joined him for the celebrations with my rebirth and my new life.

As mentioned earlier, I had already lost my sensory perceptions when things were handed over to the emergency medical staff on arrival at the first hospital. I was in a coma-like condition and was pumped in with loads of painkillers, anti-inflammatory drugs, and other sedative injectables. Moreover, at the entrance of the OT, in the holding area of the other hospital, anesthesia had already been given. Describing and narrating all these conversations, interactions, and perceptions are based on experiences that I and others involved had in reality. And I was definitely not the one whom they saw lying on the stretcher, on the ICCU bed, or on the OT table. I know it was the pure consciousness, the energy that can't be seen. It can only be experienced, which I did.

Everything was working for me for my benefit and my benevolence. There was no anxiety about the bodily recovery or the time it would take. On the very next day of the surgery, the doctors on their visit for checkups in the ICCU showed me the pictures on their mobile of the implant placed at C5-C6 vertebrae in my spine by defusing a piece of bone taken out from the right-side iliac crest at the upper thigh joint (the spare part that the human body carries to meet such traumatic situations).

Bodily, I was in deep sedation since the effects of anesthesia had continued. But I remember the chat we had and the pictures I saw of how the titanium metallic plate was implanted in the spine. Also, it was only then that I realized and understood what had happened to the body in that moment of collision. I was wondering why there was so much pain and discomfort in the lower waist area, which I could then relate to.

Doctors also scolded me to tell my caretakers to control the visitors' visits to the ICCU coming to see me, as it disturbed other patients there. I could only apologize for the inconvenience. At the same time, I smiled before the doctors and expressed gratitude for being blessed with so many well-wishers that life had offered me.

Later, I called Himaanshu to inform him of the scolding I got from the doctors for the guests' visits.

Coming back to life gave me a sense of control over my life. There was a way to achieve whatever I desired. Coming back brought peace of mind, confidence, and certainty. I could design my destiny as I desired; this belief had been set deep within.

'It's in my reach.'

It is important to become receptive to only those ideas that will bring success to life. All the resources are already there within, including the bodily spare parts as in an automobile. All the manifestations come from the way one's being is. Infinite intelligence is always pulled toward the strongest intentions, one holds.

A sculpture is already embedded in the block of stone from which it is created. It is in that very same block, and the sculptor is already aware of what's within it. The sculptor is required only to remove the unwanted pieces of stone from that stone block, chip by chip, chisel by chisel. The Creator sculpted my life into the present shape and persona by giving me the experiences I have had so far. He has everything in His mind, like a sculptor who is chiseling me so that, in the end, I come out as a beautiful creation of Him, which He has in His mind. I understood, He is working on me…

I only need to allow myself to be chiseled per His plan. I need to be fully absorbed and connected to the entire process so that what He has in mind for me blends with what I desire. And the end will be magnanimous.

All of this gave me an opportunity to search inside, to pause, and to take time out. I found unconditional love, peace, joy, and contentedness. It sounds like a dream, like a fairy tale, but it is all true, as I experienced all of it in my real sense.

If this had not occurred to me as an experience, I would not have known what would have really satisfied me, which is so deep and so pure.

I discovered myself and understood the agenda of my life. I am surprised to see myself having discovered the grandeur that life has bestowed upon me.

While lying in the hospital bed, my mind related itself to the wonders of nature. I remember distinctly chatting with Himaanshu one evening, standing next to my bed, about a tiger born in the jungles of the Kanha-Kisli tiger reserve and one born elsewhere. Even though there is plenty of food for a tiger in the Kanha-Kisli, it still has to go and hunt for its food with the same vigor and commitment, lest it stay hungry. Similarly, each individual has to strive for his own life. Further, in the resourceful environment of Kanha-Kisli, a tiger can't go on a rampage to kill the herd of deer at its whims and fancies for demonstrating its might. They are there in plenty, but only to fulfill its need for hunger and nothing else. The same is true of the responsibility of human life, particularly for those who are blessed with resourcefulness.

Dignity to the position held by a person is not brought by the show of power but by being resourceful and its benevolent deployment.

I was not in a state of crying or suffering but in wonderment.

Himaanshu reverted to me and said, *"Despite all the welldoing and wellbeing, you have still met with such an event."*

I said, *"Everything happens for a reason to each one according to their capacity and capability of responding to what is happening to them. For me, it is not an accident but an incident that happened to me, because if it had happened to someone else, that person may not have handled it the way I am responding to it. Nature chose me to take the jolt, as it found me capable of absorbing it. I am not suffering it, just letting it go through…"*

I got more and more relaxed as I trusted more and more in my power of imagination. I could see beautiful images, which brought more and more of those kinds. I lived in the emotions that these images created in me. It was as if all of it had already occurred to me; I had already experienced it.

I could hear the voice of the doctor conversing with his team or my caretaking people around, coming to my room along with other duty staff in the morning and evening to check my parameters and status of wounds, etc.

As they would approach me, my mind had already run through the entire process of checkup by them. I knew the doctor would press on my sutures on top of the head by opening the bandage and sticking it back. He would peel off the bandage on my right wrist, and press it, and it would hurt because there were still some pieces of glass inside that remained to be removed while putting the sutures there which were eventually removed by an OT procedure done 15 months later. I had already experienced the feeling of hair being pulled by the bandage he would open up. And when he, along with the team, arrived, I had already gone through all of it. My mind had already experienced it. Therefore, there was no struggle, no stress, just going through it. I knew I had to just let go…

After making me sit on the bed upright, grasping my hand, the nurse would ask me to hold the pen and write my name and put my signature on a piece of paper so as to check my sensory perceptions and brain-body coordination, which I had already practiced and written in my mind as an experience.

The doctor would ask me to get down from the bed and go for a walk on the aisle of the hospital floor by holding the hand of the nurse, climb a couple of steps, and come down, even though it was the very first day when I was moved from the ICCU to my private room.

Everyone around me was awestruck by the stride I took. I could recall the tag line from the jingle in the advertisement of one fabric brand, *"take the world in your stride…"*

A fracture in the right-side collar bone remained undetected until I complained of acute pain while trying to lie down or take a turn on the right side. It was my fourth day when an x-ray machine was brought into my room, and the fracture was detected and diagnosed. Similarly, several pieces of windscreen glass kept emerging from the nose, ears, forehead, and both hands whenever cleaning was done to put on new bandages.

On one of those days, I felt a deep pain in the center of my forehead while moving my hand there. When referred to the doctor, he, by rolling his fingers, noted that it was a piece of glass below the skin. He asked me if I wanted to go through the OT procedure or if he could pull it out right there by making a small, not very deep cut, without applying local anaesthesia. The only thing required was that I had to hold still and bear the pain of the cut he would place. Having gone through so many procedures already, I was inclined to take the second option offered by the Doctor. I allowed him to do that, then and there, and my mother and sister were in shock, observing all of this live. The doctor pulled out the glass piece and placed it on my palm, which I handed over to my mother.

There are innumerable such incidences spread over a period of close to 15 months, which ultimately led the body to recover and return to normalcy. A period of penance, when both me and the world moved at their own pace, unperturbed and unaffected by each other's active presence. There was no 'fear of missing out' (no FOMO).

This period of recovery has its own set of stories and one of which relates to certain internal complications of blockage in my urinary tract diagnosed much later, in January 2015.

This blockage had developed over a period of time. At the first instance of arriving at the hospital, a catheter was placed hastily, causing internal injury. Surgery was the only solution recommended to remove this blockage, after which the quality of my life ahead would have been compromised. Several medical and professional opinions were solicited, and all suggested that surgery was the only option.

I told Himaanshu that I was not ready for the compromise. We together decided to take a chance with the alternative therapy of homeopathy, even though all the arrangements were made to undergo surgery. This chance was taken with a leap of faith and surrendering into the intelligence of the homeopath, Dr. P.K. Choubey, and nature miraculously addressed the choice we made. This was one of the few episodes where medical science was surprised with the outcomes. For them, '*it was unusual, unlikely*', the words they used for the results.

I lived moment by moment, in the present. I developed my mind-movie scene by scene and made it happen the way I wanted it to happen, in the most beautiful way. I was hearing what I wanted to hear, smelling what I wanted to smell, and seeing what I wanted to see, all without any doubt or disbelief. In all those moments, I was always grateful for how life had brought me to where I reached.

I always got support in life whenever it was needed. It is as simple as recognizing the pillow I wanted under my lower back, the side I wanted to rest upon, the tilt of the bed I wanted, the chair I wanted to sit on, or the hand rest of the sofa where I wanted to lay my bums. Life supported me in everything I desired and kept on making me more and more grateful for everything it kept on offering me. Life delivered everything I needed. It was overflowing with good things.

I also realized that I could visualize whatever I desired in my life, and it would manifest as I tuned in to the required frequency by clearly laying down my intentions. I was ready to meet anything head-on.

The change occurred on its own. My vocabulary changed. When any visitor came to meet me at the hospital or at the residence and asked me about how I was, my automatic answer always was,

'Better than the previous day'.

I would say, *'I am recovering well. It's a new life, by the grace of God, and good wishes of you all.'*

A gentle smile always floated on my face, which I could feel from within; there was no need for a mirror for me to see it. It reverberated and got reflected by all those who came and met me, sat with me for a while, and chatted about the incident (accident for them) or wished for my wellbeing.

I learned that everyone has a role to play and a place in this world to be who they are. Nature gives an equal opportunity to every life on this planet. Each one is worthy of receiving the abundance. There is no discrimination.

It was me who had to accept myself for the way I was. I was unique in the characteristics that I was bestowed with. It was all in the mind. My thoughts changed, and I realized that I was worthy of life's abundance, which I was experiencing. My being and my destiny had nothing to do with the conditions, situations, past, my genetics, luck, fate, or limitations. It was all about my thoughts and my attention, which I was living with. I could choose my thoughts, give them my attention, and choose the direction I wanted to live in.

I recognized the kindness of people around me, appreciated the tinniest of their gestures, and expressed gratitude for whatever I received. I kept reminding myself of all the kindness year-on-year that passed by. All of this became my habit and part of me. I keep accepting more and more of myself, and in return, more and more of the goodness keeps coming back to me, making my life abundant...

My own thoughts and the attention I give to those thoughts are the seeds of my destiny.

I keep planting more and more of such seeds of thought, leading to more and more abundance, helping me to give back much more, accomplish much more, and in turn contribute to the maximum. I live out of joy, peace, and optimism, giving as much as I can. Life doesn't give me what I want just because I want it. Rather, it gives me in response to what I am and in response to my doing, which is in sync with my being.

The irony is, the more I give, the more I get back, making me capable of giving even more, and this continues…

My perspective changed, and I started thinking that most of the time, people had been so kind. Most of the time, things had worked out well, and everything was as it should have been. Most of the time, most things were in perfect order. Everything worked out well, leading my awareness to expand. And I was part of everything. I became aware of so many good things, which made me grateful for everything that was happening to me.

I decided to take my life into my own hands. My subconscious received all the information it required to enable me to achieve my desired goals. I only needed to allow it to happen by remaining aware. The only thing needed was to *'fear nothing'*. I became more and more aware of my internal experiences. I had been paying attention to my awareness, which seemed to everyone around me to mean that I was daydreaming. I gave myself permission to *'let go'*. I was eager to travel to the deeper levels of my subconscious. I was open to taking a deep dive. I took the journey, drifting effortlessly deeper and deeper for the new beginning, for the change to a new life.

If this had not happened (a bad thing as commonly told by all around me) to me, I would never have had this wonderful understanding of life as well as of *'that side'*. This incident was a blessing in disguise. An orchestrated, fully maneuvered event, designed and executed by the divinity in absolute terms. I only knew where I was headed without any control over the nitty-gritty details, which were in His know-how and control.

For me, in my understanding, the implant of a metallic plate at C5-C6 in the spine acts as a central point to stay focused, a pivot reminding me all the time to remain centered. It's like a holy pendant placed for a lifetime, always ensuring that I don't drift away.

I came out with a new life, a life with an open mind and a receiving mind, with abundance flowing in all aspects and from all directions.

We tend to interfere when nature knows what to do and how to do it. It is important to get out of our own way and allow nature to work for us. We try a lot, which in itself is getting in our own way. It is important to trust nature and surrender to it in those darkest moments. Too much of trying to work out a way from the dark does not allow nature to manifest the light required.

What is required is shifting attention and letting go by surrendering to nature. Our job is only to observe the mind as to what it is doing. We need to be detached and silent observers, like watching the flow of traffic on the road from the window of our room. The flow of traffic keeps varying but does not affect us when we are looking at it like a detached, silent observer.

Becoming aware that I am aware is crucial. In that awareness, I need to be a peaceful and silent observer. It is from this state of awareness, all that I desire comes into manifestation through universal intelligence.

Everything is just the *same* (on the outside) and everything is *different* (in the inside) as I return to myself with a new life, celebrating the new me...

What I have become, after...

It's a moment to refer

From where the past, I could defer

I am born to live this life

But complicated by creating the hype

Was chasing the world with a fight

But to bring death by the Might

I was in agony and pain

But to gain

When that moment arrived

I was happy for everything that got deprived

I took a deep dive to cross the lows and highs

In the depth, I heard the silence within

And felt the gush of love as I breath in

In that moment

I embraced life for the purpose of giving

What I have become, after

Is the moment to refer.

You may wonder how and why all these realizations, awakenings, and alignments emerged during the incident. Let me tell you, these are the outcomes of my experiential living of the past 41 years until this incident. This incident brought all of it together to explode within and create a total transformation. The present me in the now became incomparable to myself in the past.

> *Just when the caterpillar thought the world was over, it became a butterfly…*

It resembles the transformation of a caterpillar into a beautiful butterfly after going through the cocoon phase. All the preceding phases are an integral part of becoming a butterfly and achieving this beautiful transformation.

It takes a long time for change, but when it happens, it's all at once. The world sees only the most dramatic event and can't relate to all that preceded it. I realized that these 41 years of my growth culminated in all of this transformation, leading to the orbit-shifting of my life journey. This incident is a *'breakthrough'* moment that had been built up by the previous actions when all of them taken together reached the critical threshold.

Life has been full of turning points. There are 'n' number of reference points and defining moments, each one more magnificent than the other in my journey through life. There have been several breakthrough moments that have led me to evolve gradually. In the chapters to follow, I will be talking and sharing about these 41 years of my evolution, all of which will relate back to these transformations.

02

The Inception...

If I begin from the beginning, my mother tells me that when I was a baby and we were living jointly in a large extended family at our native place called Seoni, there was rationing in the family on the milk availability per branch of the family unit. She would get a quantity of milk for me, sufficient for a one-time feed only. To make up for my one more feed, she would add water to it.

When I look back, in a way, this limited supply of milk came as a blessing in disguise for me since, in the later part of my growing years, I was diagnosed with lactose intolerance. At present, I avoid taking dairy products.

My grandfather had been a grain merchant. My dad chose to study and became a Chartered Accountant. In the initial years of his career, he strived to set up his office for Chartered Accountancy practice, first in Nagpur and then finally in Indore, with no family background and without any handholding or godfathering to venture into such a professional pursuit. At the age of around 6 years, my mother brought me to Indore for my education. My initial schooling started with the New Look School on M.G. Road, which lasted with this school for a very short duration of the kindergarten phase.

In 1980, a new school opened up at Manoramaganj in the name of Sri Sathya Sai Vidya Vihar with only one class, that is, only Class I.

The most revered teacher of her time who brought Montessori methods of teaching to Indore, the late Madam Maitriya Padmanabhan, fondly called Big Ma'am or *Badi* Teacher, took up the role of principal for this new school. My dad took a chance on my admission here and shifted me from my first school to this new one.

I appeared for its admissions test. This test not only gifted me with admission to this new school but also with one of my best friends, Atul. We sat next to each other while appearing for the admissions test. Atul needed an eraser, and I provided him with one. After the test, we met outside in the school corridor and exchanged details. *We connected.* From then on, the friendship rose by leaps and bounds. In our known fraternities all across, when the name of one is taken, the name of the other also automatically comes up. Interestingly, this friendship continues into the next generation, with sons of both of us, Akshat and Archit, also carrying a similar kind of bonding who studied together in boarding school and are pursuing careers in their chosen fields. Even our spouses, Arpita and Archana are very good friends with each other.

For me, it was a delayed gratification to get admission to this newly opened school in Class I at the age of 6 years. This school and I grew together, on a year-on-year basis, in a unique way.

In 1980, it started with only one class that is Class I. Next year, when I moved into Class II, it got added to the school in 1981. Thus in 1981, there were two classes that is, Class I and Class II. This growth model continued till 1992 when I reached Class XII, adding one class every year. I thus, passed out as part of the first batch of the school after 12 years.

This unique growth model has a huge impact on shaping me, into what I am as a person today. It has made me look out for possibilities all the time, in any given situation.

When I was in Class I, I knew I would move on to Class II if I studied sincerely and worked hard at my things. But in my mind, there was no visual or physical Class II available there that I could relate to for moving in the next year. I knew it would be there when I went to Class II.

This progress continued up to Class XII when there was no earmarked physical classroom where I would move in the next year. But every year, I did. The only requirement was that I had to study sincerely to prove worthy of moving into the next class in the next year. When I did so, the door to the new classroom opened up, as if it was always there.

I learned, *"There Is Always A door..."*

There is no struggle, it is only striving, striving to evolve, to expand and to encompass, to nurture and to give. Life is always throwing out possibilities for things to happen, for marching ahead, to keep going.

I, along with my batch mates, have always played the role of senior for all these 12 years of schooling. It has been an immensely responsible role, not only for me but for our entire first batch to be a benchmark and a role model, someone to look up to.

During our growing years at the school, it had no legacy, no past track records, no history, and no alumni. We, as the first batch, were writing history, creating a track record, and setting benchmarks in various dimensions of life, including academics, sports, co-curricular, art, culture, discipline, etiquette, and so on.

Beloved and respected Big Ma'am, my class teachers, several other teachers, Paranjape sir, who took the principalship from Class VI and is still devoting his time and energy at the age of 94 as a director of the school, as well as various staff members, all showered unconditional love and affection and their blessings unto me, because of which I was bestowed with the gold medal of 'M*odel Sai Student*', in the year 1999, that is, after seven years of passing out from the school in 1992.

At the entrance of the school, on the wall, pictures are placed of past students from various batches who have received this medal. I received the award with a deep sense of honor and a huge responsibility to remain worthy of it.

I never knew that the admission test in 1980 would lead me to this honor. I kept treading my path with sincerity, devotion, intensity, energy, and enthusiasm, resulting in this recognition after 19 years in 1999. I just continued to walk the path and it all arrived. I didn't search but got the understanding that *'There Is Always A Door...'*

Since my childhood, I had an athletic physique and was good at the outdoors. In Class II, even though I was good at PT drills, the lead role to conduct the drills on Republic or Independence Day was given to one of my batchmates. I was a bit annoyed with myself for not getting the lead role. I waited for my turn to come when I would get a chance to lead. As fate would have it, on the final day of the performance, he didn't turn up, and to my surprise, I was asked to play that role at the last moment. Waiting was worth it, though I was initially annoyed.

I took the opportunity with responsibility and gave it my best shot. It came out successful, bringing lots of accolades from everyone. Photographs were taken, and I always cherish that picture wherein I seized the moment. *Carpe diem!!!*

(1982: picture of the moment – leading the PT Drill)

This lead role then continued as we moved into higher classes at the Old Palasia campus of the school from Manoramaganj campus. Ever since then, I have grown immensely in the sports arena, be it football, athletics, long-distance running, or cycling. Now, when I look back, such denials of the initial years when dealt with optimism has brought me to the present fittest phase of my life so far.

1984 was a tumultuous year when I was in Class V which happened to be the year of the state board exam. In the same year, during the months of July to September, I was operated on and treated for a stone in the kidney, at a hospital in Mumbai, another one of my NDEs.

Technological advancements in medical science for this treatment were available in a limited way. Like an open-heart surgery, this was an open kidney surgery to remove an almond-sized stone from it. Certain life-threatening complications developed during the recovery phase in Mumbai, even though the surgery was conducted by one of the best doctors available at the time and which was successful.

Acute infection had spread during the recovery period which required draining out lumps and lumps of pus formation from the body. Apart from several other medicines, two lifesaving anti-biotic injections were to be given every day for seven days to control this life-threatening infection. These injections were available only at one pharmacy shop which would supply only two injections per day since these were imported from the USA and were lifesaving. Importation was a very controlled activity in the country during that period. Every day, my father would bring these costly two injections from the pharmacy with which I was treated, apart from other medication already going on. Uncertainties prevailed during all these seven crucial days, both in respect of the availability of the injections and my response to them to come out of the danger. Everything was in a waiting mode, with each passing moment requiring grit and determination. Perseverance and staying power were the keys with which I could overcome uncertainties and embrace life.

During this period of more than a month at Mumbai, my two younger sisters stayed with the grandparents in Indore and my parents were with me for my treatment. It was a tough period for everyone in the family.

I distinctly remember those dark nights in the hospital room in which several machines kept monitoring my life parameters. My parents slept turn-by-turn on the small sofa, remaining alert all the time. At regular intervals, several times in a cycle of twenty-four hours, the nurse and medical staff would pop up in the room to read my parameters, inject several doses of I.V. medicines, and go with a pat on my forehead for the composure and determination with which I would go through all of that, more importantly without any tantrums, drama, or halla-boo. There were hundreds of pricks all over for the injections given to me during the entire treatment.

For the first seven days after the surgical procedure, water was not given to me. My lips cracked, and my mouth and throat dried out. Soft and light meals commenced only after two weeks.

Since we were in Mumbai, there were no visitors coming and meeting us during the entire day except a few close relatives who came from outside of Mumbai. I wonder, at that age, what made me cross the whole day and the whole night, quarantined in a room, confined to a bed, being all along with myself. Possibly, these circumstances must have roped into my understanding that

"There are two ways to look at it: being alone (एकांत) or being lonely (अकेलापन)…"

This understanding evolved over the years in me to learn that being alone is being with oneself, being with the existential. There is 'something' that completes the state of *'being'*. In solitude, one dissolves into oneself and goes inside. Aloneness feeds the soul. Brings the inside out. It is the connection that works. Aloneness is an expression of divine attributes.

My Master says, *"There is some part of you that is always alone, even when you are filled with courage, when you are winning, or when you are in the crowd."*

Contrary to aloneness, loneliness is a feeling of lacking something. It's a sense of incompleteness. It's a longing. In the moments of penning down these expressions, for me, there is no longing; rather, it's an expression only to share.

Returning to normalcy required the utmost care, with several dietary restrictions and regular fluid intake. Physically, the body had become extremely weak and bleak. With all this, I had to attend school as well. Big Ma'am assigned responsibilities to a few classmates to take care of me. She ensured to place a jug of purified water in the class exclusively for me and asked my fellow classmates to serve me at regular intervals and also to refill the same as and when it got emptied. Everybody had been extremely kind and caring. At home, there were several guests who kept coming to meet and greet me for my wellbeing. Attending them was a daunting task for my parents and my siblings. Several medicines and regular follow-on checkups continued for quite a long time.

(1982-83: class photograph with Big Ma'am in the center, Abha Ma'am to her left and Ritu Ma'am to her right with all the wonderful class mates)

Eventually, with divine grace, parental care, and strong willpower, I could cross the finishing line to arrive at this juncture, healthy and happy.

In the same year, October witnessed the assassination of the then Prime Minister, Mrs. Indira Gandhi. After the riots, when the schools resumed, on one of the days, while returning from the school in my auto-rickshaw, my school bag, full of books and copies, fell somewhere on the way.

It was a practice by the *autorickshaw wala* to hang the school bags of all the students on the fare meter toward the driving side. When my bag fell down, it went unnoticed. The loss was realized only upon arriving at my home. We traced the entire route to search for the bag, but all in vain. Nearing the exam, I had to recreate my entire set of notebooks by taking help from classmates, which I did without the slightest of pain. However, physical exertion was a big challenge owing to the medical treatment I had undergone a few months ago.

My teachers, friends, and family helped me cope with the circumstances. Big Ma'am would visit home to check on my wellbeing and give assurance to the entire family.

Even though the state board exam was cancelled and a general promotion was granted because of the riots, an in-house final exam was conducted by the school. In this exam, I scored second in the class and was praised by all for this achievement. My sincerity had paid dividends.

The never-give-up attitude paved the way for this milestone, yet another reflection of the facet *'in spite of...'*, to come out of a near-death experience in Mumbai, followed by the loss of a school bag full of all the books and copies and re-constructing the same to score well in the final exams.

Where there is a will, there is a way. *'There Is Always A Door...'*; one just needs to walk up to it.

Three years prior to 1984, I had fallen from the balcony on the first floor of our home at Jaora Compound, right in front of my father, who had just arrived from his office on his scooter to have lunch. This fall gave me a severe head injury with internal bleeding as well as profuse blood flowing out from one of the ears. I was rushed to the nearby government hospital. Uncertainties prevailed for two days. I still carry some faded images in my memory of the hospital ward where I was put up for my treatment and everybody was in despair, looking at my condition.

Life had to bounce back as so much had to be done, and here I am at this beautiful turn of life.

Life has put me against the wall on several occasions. It has brought me down to ground zero, but then, never has there ever been any giving up. It has always been bouncing back, a 'go-up' attitude. Undoubtedly, all by the grace of the Supreme.

I am destined to win; I am a born winner; I am the winning sperm; winning is my natural trait.

These initial years of growing had also been years of lots of learning, where I would indulge myself in learning oil painting, nib painting, calligraphy, typewriting, and roller skating. I would go to painting classes with my mother in the neighborhood, learn calligraphy with Atul, try my hand at typewriting on the typewriter at my father's office, go to the Nehru Stadium on my cycle for roller skating, and would do different activities on different days of the week.

Celebrations all along had been part of living, be it *Diwali* with my *fataakaa show* for the entire neighborhood, '*matki phod*' competition on *Krishn Janmashtami*, colorful *Holi* at *Lions' Den* with *Lions Club* members, everyday thematic '*jhanki*' shows at home during the ten-day *Ganpati* festival, saving one rupee to buy a big-size *kulfi* from *Saini Kulfi*, getting a tricycle on rent for half an hour from *Mamu* cycle stores, listening to the radio in the evening when my mother tuned in to stories in '*hawa mahal*' and filmy songs in '*binaca geet malaa*' and going to sleep thereafter.

Childhood has been an experience worth living for. School, football and other sports, co-curricular activities, friendships, teachers, neighbors, relatives, uncles, and aunts, going to the market to buy vegetables (*Chhawani*), groceries (*Kanthali*), bread and butter from the bakery (*Bombay Bakery*), flour mill (*Atta Chakki near Bright School*), the local laundry man (*Mamma Press or Bharat Laundry*), the clinics (*Dr. Singhal*) for every small bruise, *kachori* man (*Bum kachori*); everywhere, the touch points and the connect had been so enriching, so enthralling, that I cherish them in all my thoughts with deep positive neuro-linguistic associations (NLAs). I would always give to my father a proper and detailed account of money spent against what was given to me for all the above activities by making a systematic note of it.

Observing my *Nanaji* (maternal grandfather) buy vegetables and fruits when we went there during summer vacations, I learned to select the best vegetables at the best price. The *Atta Chakki* also had a library and would give comics and novels on a rental basis. While bringing a novel for my mother from the library, I negotiated with her to get a comic book for me also, which helped me in propelling my creative side as well as learning a lot.

I would play cricket with the leather ball and a BDM bat with my sisters on campus. I seldom played with building mates as I had my own schedule of activities, and they would play with a plastic ball or a tennis ball, which I never preferred.

On one occasion, I had hit a powerful shot directly at the glass bottles filled with lemon juice and sugar that an aunt in the neighborhood had kept in the sun for preparing lemon squash. All of us had run to hide ourselves, but I was identified as the one who had hit the shot. She came to our house and made a strong complaint to my father. On my return home after the initial hide-out, I was heavily scolded and beaten too which was normal in our Indian way of parenting during that time. As childhood has to be, the next day, we were back in the building compound to play the game, aunt sitting right at the door yelling at us, and we were the least affected. Uninhibited, we played...

There were times when I would go through negative emotions of anger, fear, or frustration, when I was not allowed to do what I wanted to do or when uncertainties prevailed relating to health, studies, or meeting friends, or when there were resource limitations or peer pressures. I was growing.

The small balcony of our home was my own secure and sacred place. It was my world where I would find solace, be with myself, and connect with the nature around me. I would stand at the parapet for long hours gazing at the trees in front, follow the squirrels hopping here and there, blow a whistle to match the melody of *koyal*, ponder the look and feel of passersby on the road, count the number of newly launched *Maruti 800* cars that crossed my eyes, stand with a transistor radio and tune in to listen to the live commentary of the *India-West Indies* test match while *India* was on tour and follow the 'V' pattern of birds flying by in the blue sky while returning at sunset. The hobby of gardening was fulfilled by having 5 to 6 pots with roses and other flowers kept on this small balcony. Taking care of them was my responsibility, and I loved doing it.

On one of the *Diwali* festivals, I, in the balcony, was shooting out some firecrackers. Unknowingly, a firecracker came flying from outside and fell on the bag full of firecrackers lying right near the stool on which I was standing. The entire bag exploded. Helplessly, I climbed the parapet and witnessed the firecracker show in the proximity, holding my breath all throughout. It seems, the flash of amber I had experienced in that fraction of the moment of the hit-in-the-road incident was the reflection of these sparkling lights I had absorbed on this balcony.

I relate myself to this balcony as a place where my being was. It embraced me with a meditative state and cleansed me out of my negative emotions. Thus, negative emotions could never drift me away from taking care of myself in the best possible way.

Every summer vacation was at my maternal grandparents' place, which happened to be the most exciting phase of my childhood. In the initial years, that place was a small village with a population of not more than 300 in the 1980s. My grandparents then had farmland, several bullocks, cows, buffalos, a few goats, and a horse. Village life was experienced in full swing with bathing in the small seasonal river, pulling out water from the well, going for potty in the open with a tin box of water along with some cousins, sleeping on the roof in the open sky with stargazing, no electricity and no cooking gas stove, everything aligned to nature and natural resources. Playing conventional games in the heat of the sun, soft dust of the countryside roads gave me the strength and stamina.

I would keep observing the domestic animals, connect with them, and take the horse to the river for its bathing and drinking of water along with a caretaker called *Gulabrao*. I learned horse-riding then, also enjoyed riding the bullock cart, big ones, and the single-seater, all with my *Mama ji* (maternal uncle). On one occasion, I fell from the horse while riding it when one of my notorious cousins hit its tail with a stick. This had the horse rearing and I fell on the ground. Its front feet landed on my chest but fortunately, the saddle had first come on my chest to cushion me, and I was saved.

Fighting and quarreling with the cousins who had gathered for the vacations were nothing but sessions of learning life skills. Every summer, this had been a gathering of almost 40 persons in total since my mother has 4 sisters and 2 brothers and their respective children would all come together. The close bonding, we all share between us is celebrated even in the present whenever an occasion arises to come together. Even among such a big group, I would always find my space to connect with nature in isolation and dissolve in solace. I carry very deep positive emotions and experiences of these summer vacations lived during the school time.

Holistically, life all along has been blissful, nothing to complain about, just flowing with the flow and living up to the moment, embracing the experience by giving my best in that moment. Indulgence with intensity and optimism has been the key to come this far. Possibilities always existed, and I could walk past the door that came up among these possibilities.

03

And the Seeds Were Sown...

Recently, I was going through all of my twelve-year school time report cards and found them containing consistent remarks by my teachers about me being sincere, silent, and hardworking. There have never been any complaints about my behavior or conduct. I made an attempt to decipher what contributed to all of this and got very beautiful insights.

My *Baba* (paternal grandfather) passed on to me the divine attribute of unconditional love. I cherish the way he loved me with no pampering at all. He carried me then, in my childhood, and I have carried him in my heart ever since, loving him in my '*me-tube*' moments just by closing my eyes, without any need of technology or internet.

He understood me, empathized with me, and gave me the space to blossom into what I could become. With him, I was always what I wanted to be. It was all about sharing, caring, respecting, and making me grow into what I can be. There was freedom, choices to make, and the ability to behave with responsibility.

He would do his *puja* rituals at home and visit the temples, namely *Durga Mandir* and *Krishn Mandir*, every day in the morning, carrying me all along, holding my little finger in one hand and the fold of his *dhoti* in the other, but he would never force me to do all those rituals he did. He would sit with me selflessly to teach arithmetic and let me complete my homework. He would take me to the neighbors and teach me to behave with etiquette and manners and to be responsible in my conduct. I would go with him to the marketplaces, the courtroom (*kachahari*, as he would call it), and just be with him all around, whether in Seoni or in Indore, observing and absorbing the flow of life.

With him leaving the embodied form in my early childhood, I felt missing his unconditional love during my growing years. A void was created, and I craved the love I received from him.

'*Spiritual Discipline*' works wonders for every individual. For me, there is some sort of spiritual discipline that has been working all through out to bring me this far in the journey of life. It is for sure working intensely, immensely, miraculously, and majestically in every aspect, every sphere, every area, and every dimension of this life.

There is something very unique, something very positive, something very energetic or magnetic deep within that keeps on making me go further and farther. It is 'in spite of'..., it is 'despite that'...

Having realized this, I ensure that I do not deviate from my approach to life and let the spiritual discipline, whatever it may be, continue to work, taking me closer to fulfilling the purpose of life.

On my contemplation, I could not figure out any physicality to the spiritual discipline that has been there since the time I recall from my childhood. But it is there. Otherwise, it is impossible to come thus far in life with so many experiences that have been on the limits of extremes.

Life has been a flow, but the physicality around this flow has been extraneous, challenging, and not easy to sail through. It has tested me to the hilt on several occasions, but I blossomed after every such experience.

The only physicality to my spiritual discipline I could figure out relates to my first comic, which my parents bought me. It was titled the '*Krishn-Amar Chitra Katha series*' and I still carry the deep NLA with it, in very clear terms. During my childhood, I had no words to put that inspiration into proper perspective.

I drew immense inspiration from those comic pictures. Impressions of those pictures were for me, like *seeds sown* and then sprouting at the appropriate time.

Those pictures in the comics were (and my brain still carries those images) about a child born in a jail for whom there was an '*aakash-vaani*' for his death before the birth, his parents who gave him birth themselves dropped him to another place, he lived joyfully with those who parented him while doing all sorts of mischief, fun and frolic (*ek bindaas zindagi*), a nomad in jungles with friends and did whatever his heart felt like doing, no inhibitions (*maakhan chor, gopiyon ke dil ka chor*), no fears, '*kisi ka bhi nahi, par sab ke liye*', moving from place to place taking life as it came (no attachment), reaching out to anyone and everyone, learning moment by moment from his own experiences by doing everything with commitment and a clear objective (no handholding by any teacher), always reflecting joy, energy and enthusiasm, he savored the '*potli*' of rice from *Sudama* more than anything else and returned the gestures multi-fold with no looking back, so true to himself who kept on going and going and going…

It's these childhood 'NLAs' and alignment through the comic series coupled with unconditional love from *Baba* that led to some sort of spiritual discipline, leading me Higher, Deeper, and Beyond…

I always found more comfort in being with myself, even though I had been part of several gangs and groups all through. I would always look for my spacc and would also respect the space of others. Whether in a group or alone, energy and enthusiasm are always on the rise, reverberating and exuberating.

My parents would be after me to read the *Hanuman Chalisa* and light up the incense stick every morning before going to the school. However, such ritualistic practices followed by the world around me never synced with me. At times, I would fight internally in my self-talk, resulting in mental agony, and at other times, I would become vocal out of my immaturity, which caused agony on the outside. This occasional audacity portrayed my picture as an arrogant boy, an atheist.

Once a week, *'bal vikas'* class (moral science) in the school by loving and kind-hearted Mishra Ma'am to teach human value systems and morality gave me the true understanding of '*सर्व धर्म सम भाव*' (the secular aspect of all religions). Seeds of human values of love, compassion, empathy, devotion, faith, honesty, sincerity, and the like were nourished by the teachings in these weekly classes. In my heart, I knew and firmly believed in the Supreme Energy, which governs the very being of everything.

Light poured unto me by respected *Sri Sathya Sai Baba* of Prashanthi Nilayam, Puttaparthy, when our first batch of the school went on its maiden trip there in the summers of 1990/91.

I reverently respected *Sri Sathya Sai Baba* for all the magnanimous service to humanity happening through him, but I could never align myself with the godliness of his embodied form, which was described in the *bal vikas* class by the teacher.

For me, a school trip to Puttaparthy was more for an experience, it was for being with friends, though for some it was a pilgrimage. The Almighty has its own plans that are incomprehensible, and I became a party to '*His*' designed plan.

I, along with my football coach, respected Rathod Sir, was sitting on the ground in the Prashanthi Niliyam corridor, an area designated for the males, distinctly segregated with a huge length of space from the one marked for females. The corridor was filled with hundreds of devotees waiting for the *darshan* of *Sri Sathya Sai Baba*. Among this large crowd, my sir and I were sitting side by side, the first seat in the front of our respective rows, in the place designated for our batch. Other batchmates (boys) sat behind us.

Baba arrived in the corridor, and He was in the area designated for the females, showering His blessings. My sir had a distant glimpse of *Baba*, on which he whispered into my ears to pray for *Baba* to come to us to give His blessings. More out of ignorance than out of arrogance, whatever it was, I outrightly countered him by stating,

"Why should He come to us from that far?"

The time was short for Him to come from that far and be before us since there were several other activities lined up for us during that morning session.

I sat, putting my head down on the knees, and pulled up, with several mixed thoughts and counter arguments in my mind. A few seconds later, I saw the orange/saffron-colored cloth and the feet, with my head already down, resting on the knees. My sir poked me in my side abs, and I lifted my head upward to see *Baba* standing right in front of me, at a distance of not more than ten-eleven inches. Since discipline was strict, nobody got up from behind or jumped up the rows.

My sir introduced me to *Baba* by telling him my name and that I was a goalkeeper and the captain of the school football team.

Baba, on listening to this, asked me, *"Girish, so you play football? Tell me, what happens when air is filled in the football?"*

I answered in the spontaneity of the moment, though not very clear as to what to say on such a question, *"We play football; shoot it to score goals."*

He again asked me, *"What do we do with the football when there is no air in it?"*

To this question, my adolescent mind was weary and puzzled. In my mind, there was nothing much to process about the situation posed before me.

I said, *"Nothing; we can't play with it."*

He then clarified assertively, with utmost compassion and affection, that

"When it is filled with air, it is kicked from here to there and everywhere by everyone around. But when the air goes out, it is lifted into the hands of the same players who were kicking it. Similarly, when a person is filled with ego, he gets the same treatment as a football, and when the ego goes out, he is lifted by everyone in their hands. So, when the ego comes and grows, everything goes. When the ego goes, everything comes and grows."

In that moment, I was filled with divine energy and automatically bowed down, touching His lotus feet and laying my forehead on them. The gush of divinity led to an outburst of tears from my eyes, as I could not understand the emotion I was going through. Those were nameless emotions. I was shivering, energy reverberating all around me, and I was stunned by this profound one-on-one interactive session with *Baba*, which I had negated to my sir just a while ago.

Baba drew Himself into my life to teach me, to flood me with the divine light, and to dispel the darkness inside. For hours and hours together, my eyes were overflowing with an expression of gratitude and humility for such a divine interface, me being oblivious to the entire batch, both girls and boys. They all kept consoling me, seeing the overflow from my eyes (positive tears, of course) without understanding what I had undergone in those moments of divine experience.

On contemplation, I realized I was the chosen one, being chiseled to serve some greater cause, designed for this life. It is so humbling to note the privilege of being a student at my school who had such a one-on-one divine interface with *Baba*. This places a heavy responsibility on me to walk the path in the direction in which light was shown.

I also understood that I play in the position of a 'goalkeeper' where I am thrown the air-filled football for 'their' victories and aspirational fulfillments, which I need to handle and redirect to save myself and my side. I have a much greater responsibility to be a shield, a firewall for this side, to let the flow of light spread all around and save it from such ego-filled invasions and intrusions.

As life moved ahead in building a career, adopting a professional pursuit, developing family relationships, interacting with the world to achieve success to fulfill the need for recognition, and creating an identity, in all these pursuits of worldly material life, what lay in the substratum got layered up. The flow of light got covered up, which created a sense of separateness, an illusion. Fulfillment of one need led to another, and it looked never-ending. Loneliness engulfed despite running a race against the world all around. A rat race wherein a rat would remain a rat only, even after winning. I was getting lost in myself. The original me was getting buried deep under the layers of outside-worldly interfaces and achievements.

Success was flowing in abundance, all by fair means, but the peace within was missing. Intermittently, I would come live to my intrinsic connection but again get back into the loop outside. My natural state of being was overcast by the gamut of doing.

My '*being*' became intermittent and '*doing*' over-focused.

I was working hard, sincerity was there, results were coming out beyond expectations, I was going the extra mile, I was breaching several parameters of success, and it was rocking all around, everything with integrity.

But then the touch of peace and contentment was missing. The feeling was that there was something missing and it was difficult to figure out what was missing. I was aware that there was a drift.

Fear had been creeping in, which went unnoticed. I was fearing disapproval, disliking, and being let down by the world that surrounded me. To overcome the sense of fear, there was wanting to control, which in turn was leading to frustrations, and anger, which in turn led to guilt, and it again led to a new fear. The cycle continued.

Gradually, me within was getting eroded, most importantly, unnoticed, unintended, unknowingly, without any malafides for anyone, not even for myself.

The values imbibed in the '*bal vikas*' classes remained intact and were never compromised. Fear and its side effects became dominant and came to the forefront, driving me to engage in undesirable behaviors.

Life orchestrates itself, and the way it does is incomprehensible. My Master arrives. He comes searching for me and finds me at the Pune Airport on September 7th, 2017, for the '*Aahaa*' moments.

He makes me understand the divine attributes of love as an emotion, but all in vain, as I am not ready in this aspect of my life to receive it from my Master. He kept working on me, year after year. And I know He is still working on me for the unfinished part in me…

My Master says, *"Divine attributes are always absorbed by observing someone who is already bestowed with them."*

As I said earlier, after the demise of my grandfather, there has always been a craving for receiving the unconditional love, I had received from him.

In a spiritual retreat in 2021, my Master orchestrated an event to fill me with the divine attribute of love. He called a seeker and took him in his lap, cuddled him on his head, back all over, and poured out the love by embracing him. It was a visual effect given to me to observe and absorb the divine attribute of unconditional love.

Prior to this, on earlier occasions of such visual effects in previous retreats, the thoughts that dominated me were,

'When will I receive such an experience?'

'Why he or she?'

'Why not me?'

However, in this particular retreat at that moment, my thought process was altered when He did all that after gazing into my eyes. His gaze brought about the transformation. This time, my dominant thought was,

'How blessed he is to receive such an experience, how beautifully he is being loved'...

This triggered a flow of 'love' into me, breaking the age-old psychological blockades. In that very moment, I experienced the flow of love into me as if my *Baba* was loving me. This was a turnaround for me when I understood His teaching that love is a 'giving emotion'. The more you give, the more it grows...

Through that seeker, I was filled with love from my Master; I absorbed it to fill myself, overflowing the brim. Now, the craving is to give it as much as I can, and in return, it keeps coming back in abundance…

When Akshat was about 3 years old and we were in Pune in 2005–06, once while crossing the road during our walk, for his safety, I asked him to hold my hand properly as he was repeatedly slipping it from my hand.

Innocently, he gave me a lesson in life at that very moment when he said,

"Aap hee mera haath pakad ke rakho na, bajaaye ki main aapka haath pakadun kyonki mere se baar baar chhut jataa hai." [You only hold my hand instead of me holding your hand, because it gets slipped out again and again by me.]

I prayed in my thoughts for the same *'hand holding of my hand by my Master'* to take me through.

When I look back from this point in life to that moment, I know that my Master is holding my hand and carrying me through.

It was a big day when I visited the Sri Aurobindo Ashram at Pondicherry in March 2022 and realized what a blessing it is to have the Master in an embodied form during one's lifetime, both He and I breathing the same air. Living with the teacher and his teachings simultaneously is a blessing in the truest sense.

As a devotee, I can only say:

"सुन ले या पढ़ ले तू मेरी खामोशी,

जरूरत है तेरी, सांसों जैसी…"

With He happening in my life, I know I am my Master's silent symphony…

In the arms of the angel, I feel so secure and complete. There is no wanting, no desire, no question, and no noise. I am being carried in His arms, and He is walking the path all along. Love flowing all around, being one with...

मन शांत, सुकून से भरा,

तृप्त

और क्या चाहूँ

जब अपने को तेरी बाहों में पाऊँ

बस उन्हीं में सिमट जाऊँ

With my master embracing me, a realization seeped in: '*Heart is not meant for hate but for love*'.

While creating us, the humans, 'He' poured His 'art' to make our 'HEART', and His only art is the 'art of love'.

Intellect is one of the five dimensions of life, and its attribute is discrimination. All the time, applying intelligence to discriminate leads to ego boosting. Lack of awareness of the application of this vital dimension of intelligence buries the attribute of love under the thick layer of ego.

Ego is all about me, mine, and myself. Love is all about being responsible for others and being compassionate. It's a giving emotion. By doing for others, one automatically gets taken care of.

Hate arises out of ego when there is a feeling of lack, a complex. It's a disturbance, compromising the Supreme peace. Out of my own experiences, I learned that it is the hater who suffers the most rather than the hated. A hater cries all the time, which the hated may not be even aware of. There have been experiences in the past when I indulged myself in the emotion of hate.

The sole basis had been, "*When I am right, then why me, why not others?*"

As I grew in maturity experientially, I realized that nothing is achieved out of hatred except losing one's peace. Hate is not worth trading peace. In fact, it is worth nothing.

How to deal with situations or incidents causing hatred is the moot question. I found that the answer exists in the word '*HATE*' itself.

When I expand this word by taking it as an acronym, I read it as, "*Honest Acceptance of Tragic Experiences.*" If I *accept* the *tragic experiences*, thereby meaning, taking life as it comes without trading my peace or compromising self-respect, I avoid the emotion of hate, leading me to secure my peace.

Recently, in the process of putting all these expressions together in this book, on the advice of Megha, I happened to venture into the poetic style of writing as well. Some of them in Hindi have already been quoted on earlier pages. This little poetic expression was captured late at night. The good thing was that I had kept a small notepad and pen to scribble it down. Here it is, as it was penned down:

I am writing this at 2:53 am. Am I in the flu?
My love oozing out when I got up for the loo

Everything is fair in love and war
War ends; love leads you to go that far

They say love makes you glow
'Cause it's in every flow

I am told that by giving, it brews
Beware, craving of it, screws

Love is every life's essence
Living only for its presence

It's coming out from deep inside
Even with no companion beside

You filled me with your love
In freedom, I'm flying like a beautiful dove

Love is the gift of God
Thank you for the shower, oh my Lord…

04

Exploring Uncharted Territories...

The one who keeps stepping into the unknown cherishes his return to the comfort zone the most. Staying in the comfort zone is momentary, and he transitions through the next unsettling thing as life serves him.

The journey through transitions reveals that there is the known, the knowable, and the unknowable.

That unknowable is the state of being (ज्ञान और भक्ति), whereas the known and the knowable are the outcome of doing (कर्म).

Standing at this juncture, when I look back at the footmarks left behind, this journey reveals that experiential living in this time travel has led to certain attributes of life that are now *'known'*.

Based on these known attributes and the experiences gained in knowing them, there is a knowledge that certain more *'knowable'* attributes will be revealed as I travel ahead.

However, the most fascinating and satisfying feeling that arises out of knowing these known and knowable is the experience of that something indescribable, incomprehensible, that which is *'unknowable'*.

'Knowing that I know' is the most significant fact of living a life with awareness. Deep inside, it is known but gets subdued in the worldly

living which needs a reminder; it needs to be retrieved. This is achieved by living in the present, in the moments of '*now*', the '*Krishn*' moments despite the constraints around it.

When living in the *Krishn* moment, one finds everything is there and all is in abundance. In such moments, there are no constraints, no struggle, only striving even though uncertainties and unpredictabilities are integral to living a life.

The life of *Krishn* depicts the epitome of flowing with the flow.

कृष्ण तो बस होता चला गया, करता चला गया।

जेल से, टोकरी में सवार होकर,

जन्म से पहले मंडरा रही मौत को पीछे छोड़, यमुना पार कर गया।

किसी ने पाला, किसी ने दुलारा,

पर जो भी मिला, उसका दुख हरा।

पूरा जीवन, कभी किसी जगह, तो कभी किसी परिवार,

कभी किसी के लिए युद्ध, तो किसी के लिए उंगली पर पहाड़,

कभी रणछोड़, तो कभी राधा का प्यारा।

When I studied in Class IV in a garage in the premises converted into a classroom, made of tin shade and bamboos at the Old Palasia campus of my school, and during recess or bio breaks when there was a restriction on playing cricket or football owing to a small space, to my mind, there was no sense of constraints in us in such a setup. I don't remember having any struggle there. In fact, within our friends' circle, we cherish those moments the most.

While playing cricket or football, the ball would either hit the windows of the school building, or certain shots would take the ball behind the classroom where there was an open well. At times, Kishore *bhaiya* (the caretaker, then) would help bring back the ball from behind but required lots of pestering from all of us. The school imposed restrictions on playing these sports.

To mitigate the situation, the very next day, I, along with Atul, brought a ball made of old newspapers meshed up together and rubber bands cut out of the cycle tyre tube. We had invented the game of *'hand-ball cricket'*, laying down the rules and format to play. The hand became the bat, and a portion of one of the walls of the class above our waist height became the stumps. Now, even if the ball hit the windows, it would not do any damage, or if it went behind in the well, we could immediately make a new one from rough papers and rubber bands. The pitch length and boundaries were set according to the distance the paper-mesh ball could travel when hit by the hand. And the game was created, an innovative sport, despite the so-called constraints imposed...

It was a eureka moment, in fact, *a 'Krishn'* moment when we lived in that now and dealt it with situational brilliance. The game was neither cricket nor damaging and causing any inconvenience. Restrictions of the school did not apply to this game. Win-win for everyone, nothing to complain about by anyone.

Interestingly, the game kept on evolving and became the most sought-after sport for every class during recess and breaks, among all batches, for several years in the school, even though school sports facilities grew immensely on the new campus of Vijay Nagar.

Outdoor games had always been my natural choice, and cricket came naturally to me. I used to go to coaching camps at the city gymkhana club and was among the few top-performing batsmen in those early childhood groups. This was a major reason why I was averse to playing with my building mates, who used plastic or tennis balls for cricket, and rather preferred to practice with my younger sisters with the leather ball. Even my sisters excelled in their chosen outdoor sports. Sheetal took up softball and reached the National level in her age category. Chanchal also played basketball well, representing the school team at different levels.

However, in the school at the Vijay Nagar campus, cricket was not permissible. There were several other outdoor sports but no cricket. Football was one of the choices. The school team had been formed and was representing the school in tournaments. I did not pay much attention in the initial part of the year when I was in Class VII as I was more inclined to play cricket at the gymkhana. School hours did not permit me to play enough cricket at the gymkhana. With no other option left, I had to take up something in the school for the sports activity period. I chose football, among all the available options.

There was a selection process that was taken up during the lunch recess. I was not even allowed to go through the selection and was ruled out. The selection was being done for the post of 'goalkeeper'. The statement of the selecting teacher while ruling me out was,

"Abe tu rehane de, tere se nahi hogaa." [Boy, you leave it, you won't be able to do it.]

Selections were completed. This led to hurt in me but not any hatred.

After a few months, the selection for the post of 'goalkeeper' was undertaken again. I went for the trial again. This time, I was allowed to appear for the selection test, and I got through. I was part of the selected players but was the fourth goalkeeper in terms of my chance to play a match. Thus, I had to be *'on the bench'*, waiting to get a chance to play.

The mantra explored in this selection incident was about *'channelizing hurt into performance'*. Achieving success is the greatest way of proving yourself. The proof is not for the world outside but for creating yourself and moving up by climbing the next rung on the ladder. There is no point in suffering the hurt; rather, let it be the seed for a revolution.

I reached Class VIII, but never played a match until then. I requested several times to respected football coach Rathod Sir to give me at least one chance to play a match. Finally, that moment arrived when in a match at the home ground, before the home crowd, after several hand-folded requests, in the second half, I was allowed to stand at the goalpost. In all my nervousness, I took the silliest kind of goal with the ball rolling from between my legs. At that moment, I was shattered and felt as if the earth could split, and I could submerge in it. I could not look eye-to-eye with anyone.

The next day morning, coming to school was a daunting task. That day, in the sports period, I resolved internally to overcome this and work so hard, so hard that everybody looked up to me as a 'goalkeeper'.

I worked extremely hard, relentlessly, and passionately. Within the same year, I became the first choice for the post of goalkeeper from being the fourth one, *on the bench*. The next year I became the captain and then led the school team thereafter. For the first time in the history of school football in Indore city, our school represented Madhya Pradesh State at the *National Subroto Cup* football tournament in New Delhi when I was in Class XI.

Leading a school team from Indore for the first time was a three-year effort. In the first year, we got the realization that this was something worth achieving and we could do it if we were properly trained and strategized. The next year, we went to Jabalpur at the Inter-division level within Madhya Pradesh State (MP) but lost. We resolved to clear this stage in the following year and create history for the school football of Indore city, by having a school from Indore city representing MP State at the national level, for the first time.

When I say "we", the team included boys from several junior classes, my class being the senior-most. A heterogeneous group synergized in harmony for a common larger cause. We practiced relentlessly, including

Sundays, every holiday, winter and summer vacations. Played with the best teams in the city so that our level of the game improved. Took help from several coaches, watched matches on the television, and discussed the moves, formations, and strategies.

We would enter the match with the opponent teams who were experienced, and well-prepared to charge on us, to dodge, to shoot, to kick, to hurt, to injure, to win, to flout the rules of the game. The way our team had been built by the coach had an altogether different persona and character from other school teams in the city.

During the initial moments and just before the blow of the whistle for the match, I would stand at the goalpost, a bit nervous with butterflies in my stomach, with skepticism and feeling the burden of responsibilities bestowed on me. As a goalkeeper, even the slightest mistake is a costly affair, it is fatal. There is no second chance and no room to cover it up.

However, minute by minute, shot by shot, I would sync into the match as it progressed, guiding, instructing, and strategizing. Mostly, we would come out winning with applause. It brought glory to the team, to each individual player, to the school, and most importantly to the game because of the manner in which we always played and the character we possessed. There had been very tough opponents and very seasoned ones. For our school and for us, it was the first-ever team that was created through us. There was no legacy to look back and derive inspiration.

It was because of the character of our team that even in the matches we lost, the feedback we received was *"Sathya Sai boys played an excellent game"*. We always accepted the defeat with grace and came back stronger next time.

With such devotion, commitment, and character, we were in the final match of the inter-division tournament, which would have qualified us for the Nationals. It was against a renowned school from the Bhopal division, a really good team during that time. We had the benefit of home ground. It was a tough match, with all eyes glued to our team.

As a school team, we brought laurels to Indore city by creating a historic moment with our win at the division level. We became heroes for the first time ever!!!

(1990: the winning football team – from left, Bharat, Vaibhav, Chirag, Prasahnt, Manjit, Subroto, Principal Paranjape Sir, Girish, Kairoze, Late Vishal, Pawan, Maneesh, Ravi, Nitin, Late Himanshu, Rahul, Amit, coach Rathod Sir, Paliwal Sir)

This heroism was a result of consistent hard work, embracing the pain without compromising on academics or co-curricular activities. There was always a sense of responsibility to bring dignity and glory to what each one of us on the team represented.

In the same year, I, along with three other mates from our school, were selected for the MP State Team for the National School Games, played in Shillong, Meghalaya.

I was blessed on several occasions to be adjudged as the 'best goalkeeper' in the school football segment in our age group.

At the college level, I got a chance to represent Indore University in the West Zone Inter-University Football Tournament at Kolhapur.

My opponents always thought of me as an easy target to score goals against as my height was not apt to be a goalkeeper, but against this natural oddity, I took up that post with the responsibility it required. In any difficult match, Rathod Sir would always say,

"Draw kar lo, baaki Girish sambhaal legaa (in the penalty shootout)." [Draw the match, Girish will handle the rest.]

I would always take his statement with the highest sense of responsibility and ensured to give my best to live up to it.

"Just on the strength of your trust, the world should come to peace," says my Master.

This resonates deep within me, having lived such moments through my football coach. My reverential gratitude to my beloved football coach Rathod Sir for molding me and giving me such moments to live.

The Football World Cup final in December 2022 between Argentina and France saw the magic moments of the 'goalkeepers' when one team was led by the goalkeeper and the other won because of the goalkeeper.

In all humility, I can say that in all my efforts, I attempted to bring dignity to what I represented since the post of a goalkeeper is generally taken casually, left for the lousiest or the sloppiest person, especially when we tend to form teams while playing on the street or in our residential area among the friendly groups.

This journey of football brought tremendous transformation within me to be resilient, never give up, take the extra mile to go up, work against the odds and the negatives (in spite of...), celebrate by taking victory laps, bounce back after a loss, keep patience during injuries, empower the team, own up the responsibility, have no ego boosting, be grounded at all times, set the highest standards, and so on. This had a huge positive impact on the persona with which I stand today.

Yet another historic event took place in the same year when three of us, namely, Atul, Himaanshu and I (the three besties together), ventured into the uncharted territory of representing the school at the National Science Congress, though we were from the 'Commerce' stream.

We explored and found that *'social science'* was also a stream that could take us to the national stage. We innovated, infused computer technology in our presentation during those days when there used to be special quarantined laboratories for keeping and using the computers, and made the entire project by taking real-life stories from across the city on the socio-economic aspect of the *'problem of child labor in Indore city'*. The scientific aspect of real-life data, its verifiability and analysis by using Lotus 1-2-3 spreadsheets, and its application to mitigate the problem were extensively dealt with in the project, which took us to the national stage at Baroda.

Stepping into the unknown paved the way for all the other fellow students to look into such aspects and venture into them in the years to come.

The last year of school had come as I moved into Class XII in 1991.

One may go places for growth and development. Staying connected to the roots helps one remain grounded. I have been deeply connected with my school in its entirety. It has always been with me, in me.

My sincere gratitude to my parents, who took the decision to have me study for 12 years at this school, from Class I to Class XII.

It is a milestone for a school to have its formal alumni set up from the very first year of its first batch passing out. Having experienced the school alumni of a well-known boarding school in Indore, which had been in existence for over a hundred years, I always carried a vision of having a formal, structured body of alumni of my school, right from the very first year when our first batch moved out. I owe my experiences at that boarding school to the football matches we played with them and the life skills we learned there.

I, along with Atul, made a case before our school management and the trustees of our school trust but faced strong reservations initially.

However, a draft constitution was created by us two, though we never had any occasion to learn the nuances of legal drafting. It came naturally. Even today, I am amazed to go through that creation. In order to mitigate the reservations before us, which were primarily driven by an apprehension of politics coming into the school environment, we proposed to have a 'Steering Committee' without any title for office bearers under the direct supervision and guidance of school teachers for the initial three years. It appealed, and we had a green signal.

The first meeting was held under the auspices of the then-school principal and secretary of the trust. The *Old Sathya Sai Students' Association (OSSA)* was set up. Hurray!!!

Atul and I, along with other fellow members, steered the OSSA for the initial three years, giving as much as we could to have an excellent start to it. We could organize an inter-school *OSSA Cup* football tournament, service activities like a blood donation camp, tree plantation drives, picnics and excursions around Indore, and several other charitable and recreational activities.

An incredible sense of completeness prevailed within since the *'unison'* continued.

As the road is for the journey, so is the case with life. This time travel of experiential living by telling myself all the time, *'Let's do it, giving it my best shot...'* is at the core of me becoming what I could become, unfolding the potential bestowed upon me.

Life is all about possibilities. I have been thriving, marching to arrive at this juncture and to move on from here.

Possibilities are limitless since everything is there. There is abundance in everything.

I kept walking, and the door arrived. I realized *'There Is Always A Door...'*

There is oneness, wholesomeness, and limitlessness. This sense of *'ness'* brings *'infinite'* into our very being. It takes away the limitations we build around us. The possibilities are infinite.

All of my indulgences are without any preconceived notions or predetermined expectations. There is neutrality in my mindset in the first moment of interaction. At the point of initiation, I am *'open'* to receiving. Subsequent to this receiving, I understand and then may or may not accept that situation, interface, or engagement. This brings mutual respect and foster closer ties.

The approach is secular and unbiased, with equality, as if stepping into the unknown. The fusion becomes seamless; everything integrates well, all in harmony, creating a symphony, a melody for everyone.

Yet another perspective on the possibilities and limitlessness that life poses: There are two sides to everything. The absence of one lead to the other, as in, the absence of light leads to darkness, the absence of heat or warmth leads to cold, the absence of water leads to dryness, and so on.

Darkness, coldness, or dryness do not exist on their own; they are essentially an outcome of the absence of their core element. When light, heat, or water are present, they all vanish.

Thus, what is of significance is *the presence*. Being in their very presence, darkness, coldness, or dryness is dispelled. They are all present in *abundance* and yet there is so much struggle in the world to come out of darkness, to beat the coldness, and to quench the dryness. Experientially, I learned that a little 'striving' can end such struggles.

That agony

My child, why do you suffer
When there is so much to grow bigger

He gave you the rain
Get drenched by opening the window pane

He gave you the light
To serve the purpose of the Might

He gave you the air
Don't waste it in despair

He gave you the mud
To spread the fragrance like a blossoming bud

You have all the space
Don't sit so tight, fighting that race

In my agony, I remain
To see all that abundance, go in vain

05

Doing Everything with Devotion...

'*Oneness*' defines the word 'devotion' in one word.

When the doer and the doing merge, it leads to 'oneness'. Dissolving in what one is doing is oneness. What is important is this 'ness' which is nothing but a feeling, an experience, or a state of being to achieve the unison.

Peeping into the past makes me understand the paradoxes of life I have been through and many more to come in the times to witness. Coming together of paradoxes and finding peace amidst them is achieving that 'oneness'. It comes out of devotion.

There has always been restlessness. '*What next*' has been with me ever since. Restlessness is certainly not an emotional state of negativity. This restlessness is toward aspirations, the unfolding of potential, and doing whatever can be done. It is for exposing oneself to multi-fold experiences of learning, playing, discovering, and evolving. In short, adding life to life...

At the same time, I have found myself in a state of wonderment for everything around me, for whatever I have gone through.

There are stories of getting anchored to a source of faith, surrendering to certain situations, being a fighter, demonstrating resilience and willpower, shouldering responsibility unconditionally for the greater good, making sacrifices and executing choices.

I am amazed to have gone through such moments of wonderment without waiting for a conducive environment to take action. There was no scenic environment readily available for me to plunge into whatever I could.

As my Master says, '*It isn't easy until it becomes easy*'.

My innate nature keeps me in a 'what next' mode and, at the same time, in a meditative state in the dynamism of what is being pursued. It is meditation in action, in a dynamic environment while performing an activity.

Engagement in one and oblivion to the ninety-nine at a given point in time is the essence with which everything is accomplished, giving hundred percent.

Our small rented house in Jaora Compound had a layout with a total area cut into four small rooms, a kitchenette, a toilet, and a balcony. The first room at the entrance was our drawing, living, study, as well as bedroom. In fact, this room was everything.

Sitting in front of the television when my mother and sisters would watch some serials, I would do my homework with full understanding and completeness to the satisfaction of my teachers. As I recall, I never found the TV a disturbance to me during my studies. My academic success is revealed by my school report cards. I was oblivious.

My football coach would take me to the school porch laid out with Kota stone tiles and make me dive left and right for goal-keeping practice, teaching me to land softly on the shoulders without getting injured. In the visualization of those sessions, I only saw a football, shots hit by Sir, and me diving as per his instructions. The hard floor never mattered. I was dissolved.

After the extra sports period and having gone through such challenging practice sessions, I would cycle back home, 5 kilometers away, without any signs of complaints or cribbing. I was enjoying.

Before I got my bicycle, I, along with my two younger sisters, would walk to and fro to the school bus stop. These, to me, were 'walking meditation', a term used in present-day spiritual teachings quite often.

I would go to the grocery shop called *Kanthali,* in the market of *Chhawani.* The shopkeeper there would ask me to weigh certain items that I needed on the list given by my mother so as to expedite the packing process. I would do that excitingly with full precision, and he would never cross-check my weighs, trusting me and not even watching the process, which I took with the utmost sincerity and integrity. Even today, when the grocery man meets at the crossroads, he recalls these moments every time, without fail. I was involved.

Polishing the shoes for all of us, me, my dad, and two sisters, every Sunday with the wax polish and brush (not the liquid one as a shortcut) was again an invigorating exercise for me, which not only shined the shoes but also me within. I was creating the shine.

I would wash our second-hand but original Italian model Fiat car, the yellow-colored Kinetic scooter, and the Hero cycle every Sunday with a bucket of water, which again was my very personal time. In these time intervals, it was only me and the activity I was engrossed in. There was nothing else. I was cleansed.

Every evening, setting up the *'Tullu'* water pump by priming it to lift and store the water gave me the experience of what electric shocks are about. It also made me align with the time of water supply and continuously check both sides: downstairs at the tap to ensure that water was there for pumping so that the pump didn't run dry and upstairs to ensure that storage drums did not overflow. All this after coming from school every day. There was no pain, only pleasure. I was lifted.

When we went into our own house at Kailash Park Colony in 1992, such activities increased manyfold. My mother and I liked gardening, and now that we had our own much bigger area as opposed to the small balcony, we had a large number of plants to set up a garden. Watering and taking care of them were my responsibilities. The boring-well motor replaced the *tullu* pump. Now, instead of dusting, I was entrusted with vacuum cleaning every Sunday (unfortunately, the Eureka Forbes guy had convinced my parents about the benefits of the gadget).

Doing all such chores, like playing an orchestra, gave a sense of responsibility, a sense of accomplishment, and a sense of belonging. I and the activity were never two different things. The activity was done with intelligence, and the doer had all the emotions for the doing. The doer in me and the doing were always one.

My focus has always been on the process. It is the intensity of engagement in the process that gives contentment, and the outcome will always bear a touch of excellence.

While studying for Chartered Accountancy or for commerce graduation along with Atul, as we used to study together, both of us would read certain portions of the book, turn-by-turn. Whether I was reading or listening to his reading, in both situations, I would not remember him sitting next to me. It was only the live audio that mattered. I believe something similar must have been his experience too.

But when we took a break and broke into extreme laughter, both would not know if our family members were watching and making judgements about us because we were wasting our time in laughter instead of studying. It was fun studying. In that fun, we cleared the CA exams and secured ranks in the university at our graduation (2nd rank for me).

On several occasions, Nisha and Juhi, the then office team members, found me in oblivion and completely submerged while preparing a case. I would not even know if they came into my chamber, did something, and went away.

While representing a matter in the courtroom during the practice phase of my professional career, it would be just the contentions raised on the subject matter and the cross-questioning that may come up from either side for their redressal that would catch my attention. I was completely oblivious to what and how others were in the courtroom. What a contended experience it had always been.

After coming back home from the office, Akshat (three years old then) and I would set up our own arcade of car racing, spell check, cricket, jumping and diving on the bed, screaming and shouting. All such fun was without fear, though we would keep receiving warnings from Arpita, it being late in the night, and at times we would even pull her into our playing. But so be it; we were uninhibited.

Pursuing long-distance running and cycling has further deepened this aspect of life where the energy takes over the body and makes it all happen. In these hyper-dynamic activities with intense physical engagement, I always find myself in a meditative state, irrespective of whether there is a companion or not.

Going to Himaanshu's place for a short visit would get converted into a night stay since we would lose orientation of time and space in our conversations, all relating to each other's life journey and how we can enhance our experiences to take it to the next level.

Now, in my current role, by invoking my faith, I take steps on the raised platform of the judicial forum to occupy the chair. With that seat,

I move into my zone, leading me to bring dignity and glory to the chair I represent. As I take my seat, in the gush of that moment, everything else vanishes; what remains is the document folder and the voices of the arguing counsels from either side, with me comprehending the things in their entirety and the pen flowing in speed and unison, taking notes. Physicality attains insignificance.

Everything merges, and the experience is beautiful and peaceful. There is completeness, and the results reflect these experiences. Life seems to be trained to be *entrained* all the time. It is worth living entrained. There is no split, no divide, no separation; everything is undivided and submerged into '*that* one' with the feeling of '*oneness*'...

God

While they preach,
He is out of reach

For me, going their way is a wrath
Allow me to walk my way,
And find Him on the path

They all are on the look out
See Him within,
And I don't have a doubt

There is so much He has given
Their begging should be forbidden

I plead, embrace everyone with love and affection
And find Him in your own incarnation.

06

Happiness is the Way...

I, along with a few professionals, was having *'mishti doi'* in Kolkata. It is one of the most savored and famous sweets of Kolkata, the sweetened curd, served in small handmade clay cups/bowls. Everyone finished their cups and threw them in the dustbin. I was continuing with my cup.

One of them said, *"Sir, you seem to be so happy with this 'mishti doi', I can bring another cup for you."*

I was, in fact, scratching my cup in its lower and upper rims from the inside to dig out the *'doi'* remains and savoring it with my little disposable spoon. The big chunks of *'doi'* had already been finished. The real taste lay in that dug-out *'doi'* from the bottom of the cup and from the inner sides of the rim. I licked and licked and licked…relishing it to the hilt, for my deep experience of happiness and joy in those little licks.

I could not have experienced this happiness and joy in the second cup which was offered to me. It lay in this very cup only, in those little, small scratched and dug-out sticky portions.

Having finished with this, after assuring myself that any further digging of the cup would only lead to eating the clay itself, I explained to my fellow men what a blissful experience of happiness I went through.

And these are common experiences with all of us while sipping the last few drops from the tetra pack of a mango drink, sucking through the straw by squeezing the pouch, licking the melting ice cream flowing down from the candy stick or the cone, picking up the single peanut fallen on the floor and putting it in our mouth after scrolling our eyes on all the sides and dabbing it on our shirt for self-assurance that we first cleaned it and then took it in our mouth, and so on…

Listening to a song sometimes raises energy levels, and rekindles the moments of happiness lived so far. Such moments of happiness have always been experienced from the little things, and have nothing to do with one's stature, status, role, position, etc.

In short, happiness is in the small things, nothing big is required for experiencing it. The fallacy of our intelligent mind is that we look out for big things to be happy. Happiness is not a verb. It is a state of being. One has to be (period).

Living life out of happiness has been the way for me. Happiness is the way, come what may. Having gone through NDEs with several other smaller incidents, this body of mine is *beautifully embroidered* at several places all over. These sutures on my body which I like to call as *medical handicrafts*, reflect the finesse each surgeon carried in their hands.

इन्तेहां के इन कठिन अनुभवों से गुज़रना कतई आसां नहीं था,

पर मायूसी को बगैर पास फटकने दिए,

ख़ुशी ख़ुशी इनसे गुजरने में न तो दर्द को भुगतना पड़ा और न ही कोई शिकायत करनी पड़ी.

क्योंकि संभालने के लिये तू जो है न…

मैं इन्हे झेलने में सक्षम था इसलिए उसने मुझे इन सब अनुभवों के लिए चुना.
शायद किसी और के लिए इनसे इस तरह निकल पाना मुनासिब न था.

मुझे इस काबिल समझने के लिए तेरा शुक्रिया…

Happiness is the way; it radiates from the inside and everything manifested outside feels and looks beautiful.

Let me draw an analogy.

Beautiful architectural monuments worldwide are admired by everyone without a single thought given to the skeletal structures inside them on which they stand.

If one attempts to peer deep inside, one will find those internal skeletal structures rusty, and it will be incomprehensible to believe that the same beautiful-looking building stands on that very hoary internal structure. It is the inside that provides shape to the exterior outlook. Architectural principles dictate that the inside story is the same for all superstructures. Surprisingly, these inside stories are generally considered horrifying. Having such a consideration is in itself a really horrible state of affairs.

Inside is, in fact, the most beautiful. There is no gender or color bias. There is no geographic divide. The inside is common to all, the very basis on which the superstructure takes its shape. The horrifying state of affairs is that while taking shape externally, it gets tainted with the divide of gender, skin color, geography, and so on.

The inside also requires care and nourishment. Take care of it well while paying attention to the outside. By building the outside from the inside, it will bring out equanimity, poise, and selflessness. There will be no divide on the basis of any sort of comparison and therefore no competition to fight. This leads to mutual contribution, leveraging each other, adding beauty and value all around.

There will be no room for the element of fear and doubt.

It is fear, the fear of losing control, establishing supremacy, and recognition that brings unwarranted attributes of human behavior.

When the inside is understood, fear vanishes, and abundance engulfs. In abundance, life flourishes and blossoms, beautifying the world around. Let the light radiate from the inside and enlighten the surroundings outside.

While our school team was traveling by train to Delhi for the *National Subroto Cup* football tournament we had qualified for, early in the morning, our coach and I got down at Agra Cantt station to arrange for some breakfast for all the team mates. Both of us were in slippers, shorts, and casual sleeveless t-shirts that we had slept in. Train tickets for the entire team were with sir. Between the two of us, we had little money, enough only for getting the breakfast. In this process, the train moved, and both of us were left at the station.

There were no mobiles available in those days. Fellow teammates had tried hard to stop the train by pulling the chain, but all in vain, as told to us later by them. Without going into panic, we looked out for solutions. Wireless messages were sent through the station master. We had to reach Delhi before the train we had missed boarding, by taking another faster train since all the reporting details of the team were with us. We were short of money but could convince the station master who helped us generously. With assurance on the plan we executed, we boarded the faster train and without getting perturbed, took a nap until we arrived in Delhi, much before the arrival of the rest of the team.

We were received with a warm reception though our attire and shabby condition were absolutely inappropriate for the warm welcome we had. But we were uninhibited. We were in the moment and enjoying the experience, being successful in the execution of the emergency plan. Organizers coordinated everything, and we all moved together once everyone arrived. It was a celebration, even before we entered the tournament arena. Everything was accepted happily.

Similar was the experience when four of us from our school got selected for the National School Games at Shillong, Meghalaya. We, along with other selected teammates from different schools and places of MP State, traveled to Shillong during the *Diwali* festival. There were no direct trains and no reservations were made. We moved from Indore to Bhopal, then to Lucknow, and from there to Guwahati, all throughout in jam-packed 'general compartments.' We took a bus ride thereafter to finally reach our destination. Without reservations, traveling in general compartments, full of festive crowds, had consumed our entire energy reserves. We all were in bad shape, with swollen legs, aching backs, incomplete periods of sleep, and improper meals.

We reached early evening, but it was pitch dark, being in the Northeast. We had to play our first match the next day early morning without any choice. Having understood the situation, we helped each other by massaging, using warm saline water, and getting proper meals. We spoke about what we could do rather than what we had gone through. We slept well. The next day, early morning, we were ready for the match. We played well, but they won. We were happy to have given a tough fight to the strong opponent. It was *Diwali* and we enjoyed the festivities by making STD calls from the PCO booth to our family members and sharing sweets with each other we had brought from home. With happiness all around, the pain and loss didn't matter.

Atul, Himaanshu, and I opted for Mathematics as a subject along with the Commerce stream for our eleventh and twelfth classes. We wondered why we did that, and what influenced us to make such a choice. Now that the choice was made, we had to live with it. Topics like differential calculus, trigonometry, etc., were a nightmare. Even today, I fail to understand why we were made to learn all that. Clearing quarterly tests was nerve-racking but we could manage on the borderlines.

Pre-boards had to be cleared before entering the twelfth board. A red flag was raised by the teacher. We had limited time to cope and come to a reasonable level; after all, it was the first time that our school was going for the board exam. We three arranged for a private tuition class with Gupta sir. After school, in the evening, we three would learn math from him and then sit at Himaanshu's place to practice it. For me, it always remained challenging, and I could feel the pain of facing it repeatedly. But the fun time we had together with cranky jokes and learning the complexities of the subject by evolving our own techniques made going through all that worth cherishing. The happiness in those moments can never be calculated with any known mathematical formulae.

In pursuit of my professional career progression, I moved into the industry for some time to join a software company. I had learned computer skills in a DoS-based environment and adjudged myself at a proficiency level. When I joined the software company in the Finance and Accounting function, I realized it was an all MS-Windows environment to work in. I had to unlearn and relearn to make myself productive and relevant in the organization. It was a shift from WordStar and Lotus 1-2-3 to MS Word and MS Excel, operating in a totally different technology environment.

I committed myself to giving an extra six months by staying back in the office to learn and become proficient in the technology, apart from taking control of Finance and Accounting functions. I took help from the experts, read books in the library, practiced on the workstations, and emerged with flying colors. I was enjoying the entire process. I was into it happily, and it paved the way for taking up roles of higher responsibilities as I moved to other organizations.

In the physical fitness regime, my Master gave the mantra of '*beat the sun, every time.*' I have always been an early riser.

We set an alarm at night. When the alarm rings, we wake up. However, for that sweet nap of 5 to 10 minutes, even though we have woken up, we press the snooze button. There is a resistance to getting up from the bed. This results in a time gap between waking up by the alarm and actually getting up from bed. For me, waking up and getting up from the bed has been one and the same. I created a regime for myself and happily executed it, raising the intensity as I progressed.

The exposure I received and the intensity with which I dissolved into the moment led to these experiences of happiness. Happiness is a natural flow. We stop ourselves from being happy out of being 'people conscious.' By becoming more 'conscious of the self,' we embrace more happiness.

07

Unleashing the Potential...

It is vital to work on oneself, which helps one gain control over the circumstances and improve or create the desired life. Worrying about things over which control cannot be exercised or which cannot be influenced by deploying time and energy is unproductive. I could accomplish whatever I did to create success stories by accepting what was not in my control and by focusing on those things that I could influence with my thoughts and actions.

Sincerity has been the hallmark of all my actions. I have always opted to either not do it or do it with absolute sincerity and integrity.

My father, being a practicing Chartered Accountant who had set up his office through his hard work and perseverance, always desired for me to become a Chartered Accountant and join his office to carry it forward as a legacy. However, during that phase of my life, I desired to be in the field of medicine as a doctor.

I did make an attempt to convince and persuade him to allow me to go for my choice, but my attempt failed. I then took up the CA course. There was acceptance in me. Once taken up, I gave my cent-percent to it, without any grudges and no looking back.

I cleared all the levels of the CA exams in my first attempt to become the youngest CA in Indore during that time. I did part of my practical training of the CA course (articleship) from a CA firm in Mumbai and stayed in one of the most sought-after hostels by CA students' fraternities in Mumbai, the *Rajasthan Vidyarthi Grih (RVG)*.

Along with pursuing CA, I completed the professional course of Company Secretary (CS) and a post-graduation in Commerce as well. During that time, it was permitted to take up two courses simultaneously. In a span of five years after passing out of school, with the overlapping approach of pursuing two courses at a time, I could fill my basket of educational accomplishments with two professional qualifications, graduation and post-graduation degrees in commerce, as well as an honors diploma in software engineering.

Based on my merits, I was given the post of Honorary Secretary of the College Students' Union during my tenure at the college.

Moving from an easy-paced life in Indore to the hyperactive mode of living in Mumbai matched my energy levels and enthusiasm. The transition was seamless.

In Mumbai, while undergoing practical training for the articleship, I would first travel by local train from Andheri to Mumbai Central to reach my office. From there, as per the instructions of my principal, I would visit the client sites, mostly in the Thane and Harbor Line areas. By 6 in the evening, I would return from those sites to reach the Churchgate area to attend coaching classes, which continued until 9:30 p.m. Thereafter, I would return to the hostel around 11 p.m., take a bath, have dinner, if need be, and then do a quick review of the class notes and finally go to sleep. Sunday was the only break day to cover up several personal things: catching up with friends and family, having fun and relaxing a bit, and preparing for the coming week. Everything was filled with high energy and enthusiasm, not a single dull moment.

This period of hostel life gave me some extraordinary friends including Arvind, Aakash, Vikas, Nawal, Manish, Manoj, Vandit, Amit, and Pradip, to name a few who are all spread across the globe and happily successful in their pursuits.

From the very beginning, the *Income-tax* subject took a very special place in my heart, though most of my friends pursuing similar studies felt there was nothing likable about this subject. This liking in me arose, possibly because of the teacher Mr. Sharuk Edibam to whom I went for my very first lecture on this subject, who had a unique style of teaching it, which created the interest. He had been a much sought-after teacher on this subject, both in Indore and later in Mumbai. His nephew (*bhanja*) Kairoze joined my school in Class VII and we had developed excellent bonding while playing football together. He played in the forward line and scored goals to give me cover for those I could not save. His mother, a renowned dress designer of the city, specially designed the t-shirts for our football team when we went to play at the National level.

Immediately after my CA qualification, apart from joining the office of my father, in order to develop specialization, I got associated with one of the professional stalwarts in the income-tax litigation practice at Indore, Late *Shri* M.N. Joshi *Sahab,* who hailed from the office of *Padma Vibhushan*, Late *Shri* Nani Palkhiwala, referred to as 'God's Gift to India'. In the field of income-tax litigation, Joshi *Sahab* nurtured and groomed me like his own son Manish. Even today, I associate myself with Manish *bhai* as my elder, '*Guru Bhai*'.

I also got the opportunity to experience the corporate world and reach certain senior roles. These experiences gave me a deeper understanding of the entrepreneurial approach and client-side perspective.

I continued practicing income-tax litigation. While practicing, I took up to studying law in the year 2014 and obtained the degree of

LLB (Hons.) in the year 2018, which helped me expand the horizons of my practice even though writing three hour exam papers was a daunting task owing to the incidence of November 2014 and full-fledged working office.

To keep myself abreast of the latest developments and add new avenues to professional practice, I traveled a lot to attend several seminars and conferences. For one of the emerging subjects on international taxation, I enrolled in an eight-week course that was conducted every consecutive Saturday in Mumbai. I would travel for all these eight Saturdays to Mumbai by taking a train on Friday afternoon and returning by taking a train on Saturday evening to reach Indore on Sunday morning. After arrival, post-lunch sessions would go in the office to prepare the cases listed for hearing on Monday and Tuesday. The passion to learn and grow made me oblivious to the working days and weekends; all the days seemed exciting.

Thereafter, the most beautiful thing happened.

First, a little background: the Income Tax Appellate Tribunal (ITAT) is the mother of all the tribunals in India, set up in 1941, that is, during the pre-independence period. It is the 'final fact-finding authority' and only the issues on questions of law travel to the higher judicial forums. Judicial officers in the ITAT are designated as 'Member'. The selection to ITAT is based on an assessment of one's credentials and experience, followed by a personal interview. The selection process does not include any written examination, unlike other avenues in the functioning of the government. The interview is conducted by a selection committee headed by the Hon'ble Chief Justice of India or his nominated Hon'ble Supreme Court Judge and includes three other senior officials.

From somewhere out of the blue, I learned about the Central Government calling for applications from professionals for the appointment and posting of Members. I took a chance and applied with good intent. I was shortlisted for the interview and eventually for appointment. I took the oath and charge as a member of ITAT on December 30, 2021, with my current posting at the Kolkata Benches of ITAT. I was humbled, and I took it with the highest sense of responsibility and commitment.

Arriving at this juncture and sitting '*on the bench*' has given me and my world a sense of subtle pride, which is contrary to the experience I had when I was '*on the bench*' with the school football team up on my selection as the fourth goalkeeper. My feelings have been best expressed by Himaanshu in an article titled *Creating History: From Bench to Bench*, which he shared on social media on the day of my appointment. He has been kind enough to share the same, which is as follows:

Creating History: From Bench to Bench

Circa 1988

A young 15-year-old boy was part of the school football team. However, he had to sit on the bench as he was the third choice for being the goalkeeper. The situation was tough, but he wasn't flustered. He was mentally strong and knew his strengths. Smart labour was in his innate nature. He was passionate about the sport and desperately wanted to be in the playing XI.

He decided to step up the efforts. He started intense practice with the coach. Saving goals isn't easy business. One has to grow by leaps and bounds, literally. Leaps, jumps, and dives became the order of the day. Scratches, cuts, and marks became almost permanent on the knees and elbows. These were a small price to pay compared to the dream the boy was nurturing.

After two years, his efforts paid rewards, and he was now part of the team. The team went from strength to strength and started beating the local school teams. The team realized football could be a rough sport once it started playing inter-district and inter-division tournaments.

As things progressed, he was appointed as the Captain of the team. He was maturing, and so was the team. The team had gradually become a force to reckon with in the state. The challenge was to beat all and qualify for the Subroto Cup tournament (National Level School team football tournament). Under his captaincy, the school team finally qualified for the coveted tournament, thus creating history.

Circa 2014

Life, with its tumultuous twists and turns, had made him a leading finance and legal consultant. Unfortunately, he met with a near-death fatal road accident. He immediately underwent spine surgery. Post-surgery days were extremely difficult due to excruciatingly slow recovery coupled with newer complications. Nevertheless, he relied on his mental strength, chalked a plan for recovery in consultation with the doctors, and was back to his daily routine after a few months.

Cut to the present year 2021, and he once again created history as he has now been appointed Accountant Member Judge in an ITAT Bench in a metro city.

I am amazed at how this boy keeps creating historic and magical moments. Girish Agrawal is the name of the young boy who, in his remarkable journey of life, has moved from one bench to the other through his sheer hard work and determination. He is a living legend and an inspiration to all of us!

In this journey of pursuing a career path, I flowed *like a river*, uninhibited, detached, taking things as they came, always ready for transition, becoming the best version of myself after every twist and turn the path subjected me to. I always had a holistic and not a 'transactional' approach, which led to a *flow of abundance* in all the dimensions of life.

My 'work' has served my evolution into what I am at this juncture of life. It reflects my inner being. My work is my expression. Truly speaking, it is incorrect on my part to use the word 'work' since, for me, my 'passion' and my 'work' are one and the same. I am obsessively enjoying this *unison*, allowing me to serve the purpose of my life. Working hours, compensation, position, etc. are nothing but mere details when compared to what gets manifested and unleashed from the deployment of the potential nature has bestowed on me.

Closing my eyes, when I contemplated, finding and looking for something that I could offer to my Lord for all the benevolence, I realized that everything that I chose to offer as my prayer was His only, *'nothing of me and everything of Him'*. My passion and my work are my offerings and my prayers to the Creator who created me.

My present domain of work of justice delivery mechanisms, bears only two colors in terms of its dress code. The two colors are *'white and black'*. Ironically enough, when the outcome of proceedings in this domain of work finds favor with one of the litigating parties, it adds colors to the life of that party.

When I introspect, I find that apart from the two colors of white and black, there are so many colors filled into so many aspects of my life that it is very difficult to take stock of each color with their shades and patterns. I am amazed and look at my life with wonderment, which is filled with a variety of colors, glittering, and emanating their zest with all festivities.

My life has been full of excitements such as going to college, roaming around the city first on a cycle and then on two-wheelers (*Gypsy, Ravi Kachori, Hot Breads, Lotus Hut Coffee*) with friends and later in a four-wheeler by stealing it from my dad for taking a round during his lunch hours, trying different clothes to be in the fashion including bell-bottoms and *Quadra* trousers, taking up leadership roles at the college and university levels, pursuing my career path, being competitive, watching cricket matches and movies despite having exams the next day, sensitive to pimples, hair settings with long sideburns or keeping *French-cut* beard and later transitioning into a responsible role in the family, in the profession, and in the society.

Along the way, life gifted me with several clusters and groups of friends including from the Mumbai hostel, from the college, one, for the study group, the other, for the college football and sports, another set of friends, at the coaching classes, similarly, yet another set while doing the software engineering diploma course under a scholarship program of Aptech, a group of old students of the school alumni, an altogether different set of friends with a special bonding built at the *Leo Club of Indore Main* which happens to be one of the oldest active clubs in India within the *Lions International* fraternity, a totally different set of relations in the professional fraternity at the CA Branch level, each of these giving variety of experiences and enrichments, adding different strokes of colors to the persona which I am living with, in the present.

There has been yet another set of colors in the form of being an athlete, a marathoner, a long-distance cyclist, and a founder member of the Academy of Indore Marathoners (AIM), which organizes Central India's largest marathon event.

Making an attempt to learn playing flute, learning swimming, adventure trekking, exploring the power of words gifted to me by mother nature to express myself, all these have been yet another set of bright colors that beams out a beautiful spectrum of light from the life I have lived so far.

There have been certain darker shades too, which added maturity and substance to my persona when my life was challenged by certain traumatic incidences, some of which I have already narrated. It was my will power, resilience, and a positive bent of mind, coupled with a deep sense of faith and surrender, that led me to cross all those milestones.

Another NDE came up in the second wave of COVID-19 in April 2021, which had hit hard enough to take me into ICCU for five days. I witnessed the dance of death all around, with seven deaths taking place on the beds around me. When the virus hit me, for the initial nine days I was in home quarantine with prescribed medication. The oxygen level was within permissible parameters, but the body temperature remained high. The doctor could not relate any diagnosis to the symptoms I had. I went for a lungs scan, which revealed a grave condition. The doctor advised me to get admitted immediately. Getting a hospital bed during this time was the biggest challenge, which we all saw in reality.

The reason for my state of affairs was my athletic regime. My lungs were powerful, which maintained my oxygen levels even though they were significantly infected. My high fever continued because of the infection.

The night of the tenth day when I went to the hospital from the home quarantine was spent by me in a basement room. This was a small storeroom kind of a place, which was a make-shift arrangement made by the hospital. Conditions everywhere were grave owing to the pandemic. Another patient was brought into this room and was laid on the adjoining bed. That patient died within a couple of hours, right in front of my eyes. The body kept lying the whole night adjoining my bed; nobody could take care since the entire hospital administration was under tremendous stress due to severe casualties. In fact, there was no one to look after the one who was alive, that is, me, what to expect for a dead one, owing to the overburdened circumstances all around. Everybody was helpless, which was understandable; nothing could be complained about.

I had experienced *that side* in the NDEs narrated earlier. Fear had already vanished from those past experiences. This incident of COVID-19 began with experiencing the death of another person and staying with the body in an isolated basement room. My faith and surrender were intensely qualified. In this grave situation, I was poised, contemplating the beauty of life, which loses its charm, vigor, and everything else once death arrives. I realized how life is taken for granted and wasted, unused, misused, or abused.

Death is the empirical truth. It comes when it has to come, and it is to be accepted gracefully when it comes. Until then, it's a moral responsibility to live, not giving up but adding life to life, serving its purpose, by exuberating energy and enthusiasm.

The next morning, after being with that body the whole night under compelling circumstances, I returned home. In the afternoon, with the efforts of one doctor friend, Arun *bhaiya*, initiated by Shashank and Anurag, a bed in another hospital was arranged. Arun *bhaiya* has always been very loving to me ever since we connected during the formation of Academy of Indore Marathoners. He is an inspiration to many, known for his disciplined fitness regime, positivity and beaming persona which he carries.

What a blessing it is to have an elder brother. I don't have a brother of my own so I was unaware of this experience up until this incident. In this incident, Vijay *bhaiya*, lovingly called '*Big B*' made me experience the love of an elder brother. He facilitated the entire admission process at the Hospital and monitored things from outside. The Supreme ensures its presence by all means to take care. After completing the admissions process, I went and occupied the bed. I was placed among machines, monitoring life parameters. There were other deaths during the first two days. My vomits of lumps of mucus coming out of my lungs shook every cell of mine.

Physically, everything seemed to be going out of control. Access to doctors was limited. The support medical staff was semi-qualified and partially trained. They were giving their best but were helpless in the given pressure situation. In the late night, one boy was brought in an extremely critical condition. Since there were no vacant beds in the ICCU, I was asked to move out in the other Ward which I resisted. With my bag and medicines, I was forcibly thrown out. They laid the boy on my bed and did all sorts of procedures to make him recover for his breath. I watched them do CPR kind of procedure on the boy and I felt that they must have ruptured his rib cage because of the force they had applied on his chest, as visible to me. In next 3 to 4 hours, that boy died right in front of my eyes. His body was moved out by the staff. I was then asked to move back to this bed, that is the bed from where I was thrown out. Without any cleaning of the bed, change of the bed cover and sanitization, in shock and totally wrecked, I laid on the bed. I was jolted with the thought if I reach such a condition, even my body will be treated in similar manner.

I then put on my ear phones to engage my mind in the audio commentary by *Swami* Chinmayanand on *Bhagwat Geeta* and tried to sleep.

I myself had to ensure my timely medication, nutrition, and hygiene. Awareness and alertness at the highest level were the demands of the moment. The direction of my thinking had to be monitored and maneuvered by me to remain equipped, positive, and confident in crossing the line to be with life. Mental strength was put to a rigorous test, which was the key to winning in life.

I crossed my critical phase. The aunt on my neighboring bed commented when I was getting discharged that she took inspiration seeing me and came out of the ventilator she was put up with. I exchanged my mobile number with her and was very happy to receive a call from her husband later, when she too had returned home. There was another person in front of me who had come from London and had got stuck here in Indore in the pandemic. We inspired each other and exchanged parameters to understand our state of being. We saved our mobile numbers with each other with the title '*Corona Warrior*' in our contact list. Even now, when we talk, we call each other by this title and cherish the way we fought those moments of death and made life win for us. This has been yet another NDE with an additional element of '*DE*' of third persons.

वहाँ से यहाँ तक तो आ गया,
और वह भी बड़ी मस्ती में।
अब यहाँ से वहाँ तक भी पार लग जाऊँगा,
तब जमाना देखेगा मंज़र,
जब उसके दर पर होगा मेरा सर ...

The color of my very core is that of a player. I am playing all the time. I go down every time to the arena to play, play with fun, play to win, play to express myself, play to take the game to a new level, play with intensity to make an impact, play to bring dignity to the game...

My intention is to win, a win that is meaningful, worth emulating, and inspiring. It has always been winning, and if it's not, then it's learning. There are no failures, neither in a game nor for a player.

I never differentiated between going to play, going to work, or doing anything else. The only thing that I changed during all the playing was the gear that had to be put on for the game I was playing at that moment. Be it football, studying and completing homework, preparing a project for the biology class on collecting different types of plant leaves, leading the *Narmada* house in the school, playing the role of a father in the drama or doing stunts in the *bhangra* dance at school annual functions, being the organizing secretary for a one of its kind celebrations of the golden jubilee year of Indore bench of ITAT in June 2019 wherein Mr. Bhoi joined hands with the Tax Bar for his immaculate involvement and coordination.

As part of this playing, Atul and I designed the first treasure-hunt competition with four-wheeler participants under the banner of *Leo Club of Indore Main*. We along with Himaanshu, also conceptualized the first-ever mega show and competition of Twins of all ages participating from all across the state,

The playing has always been intense and engaging.

The use of the word 'playing' has a very different connotation, which creates a very positive and cheerful visualization despite the fact that in playing a sport, say football or cricket or lawn tennis or squash, or basketball, for that matter any sport, there are more hazards to the body which is prone to injuries or casualties. At the same time, these sports are strenuous. With all such known challenges and difficulties, everyone loves to take up playing a sport, happily and willingly.

Contrary to this, when it comes to taking up work where the conditions are not like sports but much more comfortable and assured, the general perception is that work is burdensome. The zeal and enthusiasm are lost. Negative attributes like jealousy, comparison, desperation for recognition, etc. come to the forefront. Winning at any cost, anyhow, takes over everything else.

Let life be taken as a leela, a game; play it and play it well.

In this striving, taking inspiration from Neeraj *bhaiya*, who is the epitome of grit and determination for me, it was on November 9th,

2018, that I committed myself to cycle for 111 kilometers on Sunday, November 11th (11.11), a sacred day for the spiritual path I am treading. It was a to and fro cycle ride from Indore to Ujjain, and I completed it within 5:30 hours. Ujjain is a place of high positive vibrations, '*Mahaa Kaal Jyotirling*'.

I have no clue as to what made me commit to this, in spite of certain constraints that prevailed during that time, including the following:

1. I had been undergoing a physiotherapy session for the last four days owing to severe pain in my neck from the implant I have at C5-C6 in the spine.
2. ITB on both thighs had tightened as I resumed my running after a gap of three weeks owing to a viral infection.
3. Akshat was to return to his boarding school on 11.11 after his Diwali vacation. His packing, last-minute *gyan*-chats, a dinner get-together to attend, and an appeal at the Tribunal had to be prepared for the coming Monday morning.
4. My mother had caught up with an acute cold and cough and required a doctor's visit. She had been recovering from her other ailments in recent times.

In short, it was a commitment to celebrate my sacred day of 11.11 '*in spite of.*'

On Friday evening, I returned from my physiotherapy session at 9:30 p.m. and was in acute pain. I had a quick dinner. I also had to take a painkiller, which I normally avoid to take.

On Saturday evening, November 10th, I skipped the physio session owing to the birthday celebration of Himaanshu. You may recall that it was an equally special day for me as I celebrate my rebirth after the incident of November, 2014. I got home very late from the birthday celebrations, and I was in acute pain. Again, I had to take a painkiller as it was unbearable.

I changed my every day alarm time of 5 a.m. to 6 a.m. to cover up my sleep. I slept with the thought that cycling was out of question. But, since I had committed to doing something, I thought of running at least 11 kilometers, or if that was also not possible, then to run for 1:11 hour, whatever be the distance I could cover. I assured myself in my thoughts to do something with 11.11 and went to sleep.

I got up at 5 a.m. despite the alarm set for 6 a.m. I dismissed the set alarm. For the next 20 minutes, I was not sure as to what I should do. By the time I finished my morning routine, I had made up my mind to go for the cycle ride to Ujjain, at least one way for 56 kilometers since 5+6 adds up to 11. Thereafter, I thought to return by taking a bus from Ujjain.

Another thought was to keep cycling by adding 9 kilometers after the first 56 kilometers, which would continue to give the summation as '11'. And at any stage, if it became unbearable, take the bus enroute and return to Indore.

With all these thoughts, I completed my ride preparation, as I could not do any preparation in the evening. I started the ride at 6:28 a.m. by invoking my faith and prayer.

I had my God on my side, who was strengthened by my faith. I had cycled on this route only once, more than a year before, with a bunch of thirty other cyclists.

However, this ride on 11.11 was a solo one, and nobody knew about it except for Mahesh in Chennai. For any mishap, puncture, technical issue, etc., I had to be all by myself. Contrary to this, all my past rides to various places had been with some co-riders.

I started my ride with excellent speed and energy. I carved out certain rules for myself to take a break of 5 minutes after covering every

20 kilometers, to do stretching, and refuel myself by eating or drinking something.

En route, I interacted with a few passersby and encouraged them to take care of their health and fitness. Some motorcyclists rode with me in admiration of my bicycle and the gear I had put on.

I enjoyed the nature, the rising sun, fading darkness, and the sunlight gradually coming in. There were beautiful scenes of lush green farms, cattle herds, and small roadside tea shops that had just opened up in the morning.

As I reached Ujjain, to my surprise, my sports watch showed that this 56-kilometer-ride was the exact distance from my starting point to the "*Mahaa Kaal Jyotirling*" Temple.

I went into the temple premises with my cycle and all the cycle gear because of which people gazed at me as if I was an alien.

I sat in silence and non-doing for 11 minutes in the temple premises. I refueled myself with almonds, dates, and a banana.

The thought of taking the bus had waned as I started my return journey. I took breakfast of '*poha*' and later two pieces of '*jalebi*' to refuel myself with sugar and carbs.

I divided the remaining distance in sets of 9 kilometers each, which tamed my mind; I kept on paddling, and it became easier to return.

I completed the ride of '111 kilometers' with a riding time of 4:53 hours. I was back home by 12:30 p.m. The physiotherapist was amazed at this accomplishment as I took a session with him at 2:30 p.m. the same day.

This was yet another experience for me on the teaching of my Master when He said,

"Let your subconscious know that he says it and he does it; he says it and he does it."

Two very important realizations occurred to me during this ride, which never happened in so many rides accomplished in the three years prior to this one:

1. As a rider, I get a visibility of approximately 500 to 700 meters ahead of me. From my current location, I could see that far only to gauge the contours of the road ahead, whether it is ascending or descending. My mind was able to analyze and decide on shifting to the most appropriate gear combination of the cycle for a smooth flow in the transition of ascend or descend, as the case may be, maintaining the speed and conserving my energy.

This fits in so well in the *"journey of life"* to complete a peaceful and successful ride, '*Shifting to the most appropriate gears based on the current situation.*'

2. The physical resources at my disposal, that is, my body fitness level, carbs, water, cycle, various gears and gadgets, energy to paddle, compass, GPS watch, etc., were all available and were used to the optimum.

Still, it was the road, the path, and the optimum deployment of resources that led me to the desired objective of fulfilling a purpose. *It's the road, the path,* that gave direction to the entire deployment of various resources, which otherwise would have been directionless and meaningless.

On this wonderful accomplishment of my cycle ride, I realized that something since childhood has been working right. It seems my '*magnet*' had been set right, which attracted all the desirable things. I find myself blessed for the life so far, attracting '*Best-in-Class*' in almost every aspect of life.

In my pursuit of health and fitness regimen, for marathon running and long-distance cycling, I am extremely grateful to have been intimately surrounded by ace athletes including Neeraj *bhaiya*, who has to his credit, accolades for completing cycling from Kashmir to Kanyakumari (North-South) and also from Dwarka to Dibrugarh (West-East) along with several such incredible events; Sudarshan, who is the first person in the central India to complete 12 consecutive full marathons in 12 different cities in 12 months; Vijay *bhaiya*, an elite runner who got into running at the age of 57 and completed the *Comrades* Ultra-marathon (89 kilometers) in South Africa; Rajeev *bhai* who has been a pacer for the Airtel Delhi Half Marathon; Abhishek who is an avid adventurist trekking several mountain peaks; and many more. All these incredible achievers are fine human beings, great source of inspiration, and they led me to higher levels by holding my hand all the time.

During my career development phase, I could not remain an active sportsperson but resumed it actively 2010 onwards. However, after the incident of November, 2014, I was advised by the doctors to avoid sports that required sharp reflex movements. I had asked the doctors for the alternates available, and they, having understood my obsession, hesitatingly advised me only to run, cycle, and swim in a limited way.

In fact, my first question to the doctors when they came for my check-up in the room at the hospital was to understand if I could continue with my physical fitness activities. There was not even an iota of doubt or disbelief in my mind about my recovery. In that grave condition also, I was looking at my future with optimism, and they were all astonished by it.

From the advice of the doctors, running was my first choice. I had done my first half marathon in Mumbai in January 2013 followed by another in January 2014 both of which were before the occurrence of my incident. I could not take up the one in January 2015 as I was bedridden, although I had registered for the event beforehand. Since I missed this event, I resolved to recover myself from the incident with a targeted approach so that I could take up the challenge of completing the January 2016 event.

During this time frame from November 2014 to February 2015, I was absolutely bedridden with a Philadelphia collar fixed all around my neck. For the neck region, this collar acts like a plaster which is put for a bone fracture. I had several other infection issues that had come up later after I was discharged from the hospital. With this collar on my neck, lying down and going to sleep in itself was a nightmare. Getting out of bed and using the toilet at night was also a risky proposition for me. It was the winter season, and covering my head and ears was also a daunting task. My niece, Ayushi (daughter of Chanchal) would come to my bed in the night once I had lied down by taking the assistance and she would say,

"Chalo, Mamaji ko ek sunder flower banaa deti hun." [Come, let me make Uncle into a beautiful flower.]

She would then wrap my head and ears by putting a shawl curled up from one shoulder to the other shoulder giving it a shape of a flower. I cherish these beautiful moments.

In my recovery phase after I was discharged from the hospital, as I had resolved within myself for the January 2016 Mumbai half marathon, my preparation started with getting up on the bed and then getting down from the bed, moving on my own to the toilet, then moving within the house from one room to another, then walking in the porch area, then walking in the street in front of the house, then going to a nearby park for a walk, crossing all these milestones, one after the other, took a little over six months. My physiotherapist, Dr. Shroti, worked intensely and relentlessly for me and with me. Going through all those painful movements and exercises called for a tremendous level of commitment and patience on both sides, physio and me. I willingly went through all of it embracing the pain but without any suffering because pain was inevitable but suffering was avoidable.

Subsequently, I shifted to jog-walk-jog-walk movements. After hitting the running track, there was no looking back. On January 17th, 2016, I was standing at the starting line of the Mumbai Marathon (15 months after the incident with an implant at C5-C6 in the spine), and *positive tears were rolling out from my eyes*. I carried two five-hundred-rupee notes in my pocket while standing on the starting line of the marathon as I had assured my family and friends that, in no case would I risk my body and would exit at the slightest discomfort, take a taxi, and return to the hotel. I knew I would go as far as I could, and after arriving there, I would go further, and so on.

I was there at the Mumbai marathon in January 2016 to test myself and to prove myself. Every step, every breath, every drop of sweat, every sip of water, every gaze of the passing runner was enthralling, reverberating…

As I was approaching the finish line, I looked up in the sky, thanked Him for the blessings. I then *crossed it* with humongous pride within myself.

After finishing my half marathon, in the holding area there, I stood before a mighty poster of the great and inspirational runner *Shri* Fauza Singh (the first 100-year-old person to ever run 26.2 miles, that is, 42 kilometers) and took a picture there. I sat there in silence, soaking in the energy.

(17 January, 2016: a proud finisher – Mumbai Half Marathon)

On my return to Indore after running and finishing the Mumbai half marathon, to express my gratitude, I met the doctors who had operated on me and narrated the entire experience to them. According to them, my entire incident, my recovery therefrom, and getting back on track to such an extent were all *unusual in medical science*, as the exact phrase used by them.

One of the two doctors mentioned that he was writing a book on the top 100 positive cases he had dealt with, and my case, according to him, was one of the top two, the other being of a lady who had come out so well, defying the *'known'* medical parameters. In the entire conversation, they avoided using the word 'miracle', which I could understand, they being medical science persons. But I could unhesitatingly and with utmost gratitude say, that life had been all miracles, nothing else.

I told, *"I am having 'an affair' with life."*

I came out and sat in my car in silence, with positive tears rolling out from my eyes.

Silence...

And I realized; silence is not something you do but it's what you are...

Silence is about being...

It is not an activity, it's with which all the activities are done...

In silence, I danced with exuberance...

In silence, I laughed my heart out with me rolling here and there...

In silence, I cried with an outburst of positive tears...

In silence, I spoke loudest to myself...

In silence, I fought the toughest fight within to lead me one notch up...

In silence, I am with You, in You...

Thank You so much for filling me with You and Your silence...

Silently Yours.

My recovery phase continued, and I took up the challenge of completing a cycling event called *Brevets De Randonneur Mondiaux* (BRM) 200 kilometers to celebrate the second anniversary of the incident that led to my rebirth. This BRM distance is supposed to be covered by the cyclist in a fixed given timeframe to claim a certificate and a medal. The date for this event was November 7th, 2016, and the route included the spot where the collision had taken place. These two factors were more than enough to motivate me to take up the challenge.

By doing this, I wanted to feed my subconscious with positive visualizations and emotions of traveling on road without any fear and apprehensions. There were a few well-trained riders and many first timers like me to take part in this BRM 200k.

While cycling, the shoulders of the cyclist have to bear a good amount of load since both the hands are rested on the crossbar. Additionally, to keep the body posture aerodynamically aligned, the neck somewhat protrudes in the front. This was an extremely difficult posture for me to get used to for cycling for 12 hours at a stretch to cover a distance of 200 kilometers. Another set of physiotherapists, including Mr. Raghuveer and Mrs. Soni, worked on me to bring strength to the upper back region of my body by applying a variety of methods and techniques. I underwent several sessions with them who worked intensely on my body.

I was extremely excited at the flag-off of the BRM 200k cycling event and started very well. I took a break at Dewas to refuel with *dosa* and coffee. An ace cyclist Prashar ji, fondly known as *Pary Paji* who had already done 600 kilometers BRM accompanied me in the initial hours for ice-breaking and gave the confidence to take the event head-on with fun and enjoyment. By afternoon, I reached the midpoint, Dodi, between Indore and Bhopal and I started returning back to Indore.

Fellow riders decided to take a break for lunch and recovery, though my mind was focused on touching that 'spot' which was yet to arrive. I remained with the group of cyclists, finished lunch quickly, did a few stretching exercises, and marched on.

Based on the records of the incident, I was able to identify the nearest village. I had an image of the surroundings of that 'spot,' which I had captured in the wee hours of that morning. My brain was simultaneously mapping the surroundings as I pedaled slowly when I arrived at the village. I figured out the 'spot,' got down from the cycle, stood there with eyes closed, prayed in those moments, and expressed deep reverential gratitude to the Supreme.

While standing at that 'spot,' of the occurrence of the incident, I said to myself in the voice inside which was loud and clear within,

"I was brought down right here and was broken into pieces, but here I am after bouncing back with resilience and willpower, embracing life. I will not give up, I will rock and yes, I can..."

With eyes welled up with positive tears, I moved on for the remaining part of the ride, so as to return back to Indore. Before leaving that spot, I took a picture of the proud moment I had experienced.

(7 November, 2016: acknowledging the Supreme at the spot of the 'incidence', midway while cycling 200km BRM)

I arrived at Indore in the evening, completing the event successfully in a little over 12 hours, cementing my belief in life and deepening my faith in the Almighty. Yet another miracle...

08

Music in My Life…

Life is music… it starts with the very first beat of the heart—*dhak-dhak, dhak-dhak*. It's an odyssey of rhythm.

हर सांस एक लयकारी में बद्ध है.

उसमें सुर है, लय है, ताल है, उतार और चढ़ाव है, नियम बद्ध है पर फिर भी पूरी स्वतंत्र है, न कोई धर्म, न जात पात, न देश परदेश, इसमें गति भी है और ठहराव भी.

सा से शुरू और सां पर ही अंत, संगीत तो ब्रह्म नाद है, न आदि, न अंत, सिर्फ अनंत.

संगीत तो ऐसा माध्यम है जो जुड़ता है, जोड़ता है, और जोड़े रखता है.

संगीत की जुबां सही मायने में केसरी जुबां है,

हर एक पर अपना रंग छोड़ देता है, खुशबु के साथ एक अमिट छाप.

वह तो जादू भी है और परम सत्य भी.

Music is eternal and universal, flowing all throughout. It flows from the inside out. Through the senses, it touches the heart and soul, purifying them. It's a cleansing agent, a purification process. Music is the language of the soul; it is divinity in the flow. Music is in me and through me. I am just an instrument of Him letting the eternal flow continue.

Like music is a "flow," same is the case with my life which has always been in a flow, ever since my childhood. During my childhood my mother would regularly tune in to *Binaka Geet Mala* and then *Hawaa Mahal* programs on the radio, and I would slip into my sleep, listening to them with her.

My father always got the latest technology gadgets, be it the Sony two-in-one cassette player and recorder, the Kodak camera, the black-and-white television or the color one, the VCR, and so on. Keeping himself "future-protected" for a reasonably good period of time had been the hallmark of his decisions while buying such electronic gadgets. With the Sony two-in-one player and loads of audio cassettes, both old *Hindi* songs and *bhajans* were regularly played by him.

Since my early childhood, I had grown as an excellent listener, enjoying music in its various forms. Even at my school, the everyday morning prayer included the singing of *bhajans* after the chanting of *Omkar*. However, I had strong inhibitions about going up on stage and taking up this art form of singing. Nobody ever promoted or encouraged me to take it up and learn it. There was an internal urge in me to take up and learn playing a musical instrument. As I recall, initially I was attracted to mouth harmonicas. I got one such piece of mouth harmonica as a gift on one of my early birthdays, but I could not learn to play it; it always remained kept in the drawer of my study table. My urge then shifted to take up to learning the flute, but that also remained dormant.

I had always been a big fan of the legendary all-rounder Kishore Kumar *Sahab*, and during my adolescent phase of life, I had a huge collection of his song albums in the copied versions of audio cassettes, which I recreated through one of my school classmates, Ravi. In all his songs, it was the lyrics that drew my attention more than the music. Listening to the heart-touching lyrics of these several beautiful songs kindled emotions and feelings within me, and I would contemplate on them or relate them to my life situations and experiences.

I do not understand the technicalities and nuances of music in respect of its *sur, taal, raag, gharaanaa*, etc., but my heart and mind are automatically drawn towards the soul-touching musical notes irrespective of the language and the singer.

I married Arpita, a girl to whom nature has gifted a melodious voice, a divine blessing to her. Dr. Karnawat, an ENT surgeon and a friend, always says, whenever we get a chance to meet him, that the melody in voice comes only by divine grace and cannot be learnt or acquired. Arpita is fortunate to have received this grace from the divine. She has done a six-year Master's course called *Sangeet Visharad* in Indian classical vocal music. She is also a good reason for me to enhance my listening skills, making me a good audience.

Within me, I had always held a desire that at some point in life, I would give a fair try to learn the art form of music. Incidentally, I got a chance to connect with one excellent teacher in the year 2012 at Indore while coordinating a musical night program which Anish *bhaiya* and I had conceptualized for the *Leo Legends Club*. This program was scheduled around the '*rakhi*' festival time and therefore was titled '*Sur-Bandhan*', in which *Pt. Shri* Gautam Kale *ji* and his team mesmerized the club members in the audience with their beautiful and soulful singing. From this very first interface with *Pt. Shri* Gautam Kale *ji* because of this program, a very special connection sparked between us, which is live even today.

However, it was only after seven years, in October 2019, that I went to him to make an attempt of learning vocal music. He was kind enough to let me in his music classes and he worked hard on me to make me learn the same, but after putting in sincere efforts I realized to continue to be a good listener and enjoy the music.

In December 2021, I moved to Kolkata owing to my work. My desire to learn music had remained unfulfilled. With the help of one office team member, Shamik *ji*, I got connected to a flutist, Deepayan *ji*, who would come once a week and teach me to play the flute. I again made my sincere attempt to address the incomplete cycle of my childhood to learn playing a musical instrument. Since August 2022, under the guidance of the teacher, I have been making sincere efforts to get to at least the basics of playing the flute.

Getting into learning the art of music has made me immensely grow in the respect and admiration I had been carrying in my heart for the legendary maestros of music, be it vocal or instrumental. I have been blessed to attend and be a part of several live performances of a large number of legendary maestros like *Pt.* Bhimsen Joshi, *Pt.* Jasraj, *Pt.* Hariprasad Chaurasia, *Ustad* Zakir Hussain, *Ustad* Rashid Khan, *Pt.* Shivkumar Sharma, *Ustad* Amjad Ali Khan, *Pt.* Ronu Mojumdar, *Gaan Saraswati* Kishori Amonkar, *Begum* Abida Parveen, *Begum* Parveen Sultana, and *Ustad* Taufiq Qureshi, naming some of them with utmost humility at my end.

Whenever I experienced such legends performing live, they always inspired me to grow to a similar stature in the domain of my potential that nature has bestowed upon me. I always acknowledged and appreciated their *'effortlessness'* which they would have achieved through their relentless and Herculean efforts, not visible to the world outside.

I owe a part of me to them for where I am today since they have been an immense source of inspiration for me to achieve the same *'effortlessness'* in my domain of work/passion, which, as I understand, comes only by putting in incomprehensible and unperceivable efforts.

Whatever I took up to learn or develop into, I always took it wholeheartedly. Such pursuits of mine had definitely not been to impress or show off, especially in the adolescent phase of life when there is a strong natural urge that flares up to create one's identity. For me, it has always been to express myself, to be the best version of myself in whatever I took up for my pursuit.

By nature, I am a shy person. To venture into anything, initially I would struggle internally to overcome the shyness and after overcoming it, plunge in to express the same to the best of my ability. This initial inhibition and then exploding to the maximum continues even in the present times when I venture into anything new. In all such pursuits, I don't know whether I wanted to prove it to myself or to the world, but I kept doing it and kept growing, with abundant success flowing in.

In the performing arts segment, at the school level, I took part in dramas, plays, and skits with whatever role I was given by the teachers. There had been a flow, and I had been flowing with the flow.

As a parent, I find that Akshat is keen to take performing art forms in the fields of theater, drama, and screen to serve the purpose of his life. The best thing that has come up so far from him in this aspect of his life is that he is a choice-maker with strong self-belief, despite a lot of resistance in his concentric circle of relationships. Filled with strong belief, he is yet to begin his journey on his chosen path. For his belief, in my thoughts, I hold what my Master says:

"Belief at the beginning of the journey defines the journey."

I get enthralled when I see parent-child duos like *Ustad* Alla Rakha and his son *Ustad* Zakir Hussain, Amitabh Bachchan *Sahab* and his son Abhishek, Javed Akhtar *Sahab* and his son Farhan, Kaifi Aazmi *Sahab* and his daughter Shabana Azmi, Dhirubhai Ambani *ji* and his son Mukesh, and Sudha Murthy *ji* and her daughter Akshata.

Akshat, our only child, turned 21 in November 2023. Our relationship as father and son has been growing lovingly. In him, I have found one of my best friends in life, and our relationship keeps evolving wherein both of us keep growing. He reciprocated with openness, and along with him even his friends have become my friends.

We would sit together and chat for long hours, sharing our views, whether we agreed or disagreed with each other. Even if there were rantings between us, we were aware that it was for the good, to vent out and get released without making any judgement or creating any misunderstanding about the ranting done. We indulged in talking about dreams and future prospects, understanding our passion and potential to work on. At times, he would correct me for my notions, and on other occasions, I would point him out for doing certain exercises and practices for his wellbeing, be it physical, vocabulary-related, about his thought process, spirituality, social behavior and so on. We would talk about several things, various perspectives of life, delve on them, and figured out what best worked for us.

At times I would take him for a run early in the morning, and on other occasions, he would take me for a long drive in our *'bluetiful'* *Ford Eco Sport*, with him in the driving seat, both for the car and the impromptu discussions we would indulge in. We would laugh our hearts out at the silliest of things happening around us and enjoy those experiences.

Like any other parent, I love to give everything of myself unconditionally for his wellbeing without any attempt at pampering, which he takes up with the utmost sense of responsibility. We both have grown immensely in this relationship and cherish every moment of being together. All of this had a wonderful impact on my persona; from craving to receive love, I became a giver of this vital attribute of life.

From the parenting perspective, Arpita and I have always dreamt of contributing our child as a good citizen to the world. We take pride in the way Akshat has come up at his age and is making efforts to mark his presence by harnessing his potential in the performing art segment, and at the same time is deeply rooted in the spiritual dimension of leading a holistically abundant life.

From my own upbringing, as I grew up, an understanding synched deep within that a child born through the parents is for the world; it is a trust that nature has bestowed on the parents to nurture the child with love and enable him to blossom to his potential with his own aspirations, ideas, and thoughts. My understanding is inspired by the beautiful expression by Khalil Gibran in the book '*The Prophet*' that,

"Your children are not yours, these are the trust of life, give them your love but not your thoughts because they have their own ideas…"

There is so much wanting within, to give as much as I can to the world around me. For love, now I know, it's all about getting by giving. Thank you, my Master, for this realization. Life is a continuum, flowing like a perennial river, moving in rhythm with the exuberance of energy and enthusiasm, reaching out to the world to give as much as one can. Let my life be the one where I am able to contribute as much as I can, and become as useful as I can; let me be the instrument for the flow of music all around.

Ila Ila ooo...

My boy got cranky
For he wanted a Frankie
Ila Ila ooo…
He said, arey mujhe dila do

For the candy, he rumbled and fumbled
Pulled the crowd all around to be humble
Ila Ila ooo…
They all said, arey usko dila do

Struck the thunder light
With pampering, life will be a fight
Ila Ila ooo…
My lord said, tough love usko de do

Ila Ila ooo…
Bas fir kya
Usne mere dil ko liya chhoo

09

Giving and Getting...

Dreams have been the hallmark of my life lived so far. I have lived with dreams that have never let me sleep.

I dream as if I am awake in the sleep itself, visualizing what I need to do in my life and serve its purpose. In different phases of my life, as I recall, there had been dreams relevant to that phase. In those phases of my life, they were very difficult to comprehend and achieve but were eventually achieved. *Thy will prevails...*

Ever since my childhood, as a *'team player'*, I always aspired to be in a leadership role. Not that I wanted to command or control by taking up the leadership role, but to empower them to unleash their potential.

Various leadership roles I have already spoken about have given me several opportunities to work with various teams to empower each member of those teams to optimize and maximize the potential bestowed upon them. I only played the role of an enabler, as a catalyst, which led to the growth of everyone. I was aware and willing to be as useful as I could to the world to bring positive transformations in whatever way I could.

I dream of being *'a giver'*, to give as much as I can for the humongous bounties I have received so far from nature. In this life, even if I am able to inspire at least one individual for their growth, I will consider it the fulfillment of my dream.

As one more step toward fulfilling the dream of being a giver, the cosmos brought this alignment into my life, allowing me to express my thoughts, feelings, and life experiences through the power of words, and here I am expressing myself through 'Wonders of Words'.

'*Wow*', what an alignment!!!

The commonly used phrase '*give and take*' has always perplexed me, as against my preference of replacing it with '*give and get*'.

Giving, which is common in both the phrases I stated, is an act of providing or offering someone something. It is executed by our free will and zeal to part with something for the other, to whom it is given. There can be occasions when the act of giving is done without the willingness of the giver, which can at best be termed, fulfilling the obligatory duty imposed upon the giver.

Based on my experiential understanding, the phrase '*give and take*' sounds like a transactional approach. In this phrase, the act of '*taking*' need not always have the attribute of willful parting at the end of the person from whom it is taken. Such taking from the other person might be out of force, compulsion, non-acceptance, and similar negative aspects. This act of taking appears to be unilateral; the person giving only takes, with the other one remaining passive. It doesn't seem to be participative and inclusive but more authoritative, dominating, purely transactional in nature, devoid of feelings and emotions.

On the contrary, '*give and get*' reflects otherwise, since for a person to get, the other one has to perform the same act of giving. It is bilateral. It involves the other, and the attribute of willingness is built into such an interface. Getting is nothing but receiving.

Giving and getting is a win-win solution.

If minutely observed, even the body language, that is, the movement of the hand, is different in the act of 'taking' than while 'getting'. You may close your eyes and visualize the two acts to understand and feel the difference between the two.

As I understand, in the journey of life, giving first and then getting, or the other way around, that is, getting first and then giving, what precedes the other is insignificant.

I always participated in the service activity of *'Narayan Seva'* in the school, done every year on the birthday celebration of *Sri Sathya Sai Baba* on November 23rd. One meal was required to be brought from home by all the students, which was collected in the school to feed the needy and poor. The essence of the service had been *'maanav seva hee madhav seva hai'* [service to man is the service to God]. This service was an act of worship for me.

At home, my mother would prepare the first *chapati* for the cow, and the last one for the dog. In my childhood, she would ask me to go and feed them with this. The wheat flour was spread around the ants in the small balcony. Some grains were also kept on the parapet of that small balcony for the birds. All this gave me blissful moments.

On one of the cold winter nights on the occasion of the New Year, my mother and I went out with a good number of new blankets to distribute to people sleeping on the roadsides, shivering and pained by the chill winds blowing. I ensured that my mother was well covered with warm clothes before we took up the venture of hunting these needy people on the dark streets of the city. On the chilling winter night, I drove for more than 50 kilometers looking for such people. We would get down, take the brand-new blankets, uncover the person from whatever they had managed to cover themselves with, and then spread the blanket on them. Shockingly, we found people had covered themselves with newspaper, polyethylene or plastic bags, cardboard, and so on.

These visual glimpses brought tears into our eyes and, at the same time, a feeling of contentment that a deserving person got what was needed through us. We became an instrument for bringing some comfort to them. Some cried, some thanked, some folded their hands, and some raised their hands to give blessings. We returned home around 2 a.m. that night, overwhelmed by the depth of satisfaction we experienced.

Attending any call for blood requirements, subject to me fulfilling the medical parameters, had never disturbed me, whether post-midnight from the neighbor or during working hours from Himaanshu for his office colleague or for a relative of a friend of a friend at a far-off hospital. All calls were attended. Several blood donation camps under various forums such as that of my alumni, the Leo Club, etc. were also arranged regularly, with large participation from the general public. Donating old clothes, shoes, and notebooks, giving lifts on the road, creating plantation drives, raising awareness about avoiding tobacco, creating drives for physical fitness, especially among the youth, and several other such acts had always been part of this blessed life.

For me, it is not about doing charitable activities; rather, it is about the mode in which life is being lived. This mode is achievable by acts as simple as pulling up a chair for a fellow professional in the courtroom, temporarily sharing my black tie or my black coat to the counsel who had not come in the prescribed dress code, and assisting another counsel in the middle of his arguments by passing on a note to him containing relevant judicial precedents for defending the matter he was representing in the courtroom.

In my professional journey, I got connected with a fellow CA professional, Hitesh, in the courtroom one of the days. Lots of mutual sharing occurred since he had worked with one of the stalwarts of the income-tax litigation practice domain, as I did in my initial phase of career progression. During the incident in November 2014, since I was bedridden for more than 6 months, office activities were severely hampered. Hitesh took charge of the office voluntarily and devoted his time and energy by physically being at our office. Every day, he would visit me and give updates on what had transpired. On this experience of Hitesh while being at our office, he in a humbling manner acknowledged of getting inspired and understanding what it was to have one's own office. Later, he ventured to set up his own good office. In reciprocation, I acknowledged him for the inspiration I got from him to create a well-furnished office facility, which I experienced from the setup of his own office. We both cherish mutual inspiration and acknowledgment between us.

Similarly, while doing a specialization course in Mumbai in 2012 for eight weeks on consecutive Saturdays, I connected with yet another CA professional, Digesh, who had been an expert in that subject. We had developed a good volume of professional work in that domain in the local geography of Indore after our connection. He, along with other colleagues, traveled from Mumbai in November 2014; even though it was a phase of peak workload for them in their office at Mumbai. They stayed in Indore for more than two weeks to ensure all the professional filings of several clients on the specialized segment of work we had developed together. With the presence and efforts of Digesh and his team, all the commitments of servicing the clients were met without any default, even after me being in a critical phase during that time.

Keeping things in their place, being organized and meticulous, ensuring quality and punctuality, fulfilling the commitment, avoiding excuses, and owning up to responsibility are all part of contributing to the benevolence of the ecosystem in which one operates.

Atul, Himaanshu and I, depending on our mutual availability, would participate in several public events of different genres taking place all across the city, be it a mango festival, a rose exhibition, a book show, a tribal and cultural fun fare, or visiting new eating joints. We enjoyed being part of the buzz around, observing and absorbing life in a celebrative mode.

It was this trait of mine that led me to have my first interface with my Master on His visit to Indore on June 22nd, 2013, for a two-hour life-transforming session delivered by Him at the *Ravindra Natya Grih* Auditorium on the subject '*Life of This and That*'.

That morning, the newspaper had a coupon printed therein that was to be brought to the venue for attending this session by my Master. In the morning itself, I had called Himaanshu to take out the coupon so that we two could go for it. Punctuality had been our trait; we arrived on time, were in the queue, got the entry, and were seated in the auditorium. *For we two, it was a natural flow of getting inside, all peacefully.*

I was aghast and awestruck to note the '*on-dot*' commencement of the session. It took a few seconds to get in tune with the energy I witnessed on the stage. Every single word delivered by Him went deep within, along with the energy they carried. I was again in wonderment when it ended '*on-dot*'. This session was more of an '*intellectual delight*' for me; the spark of spiritual connection did not ignite. As I moved out of the auditorium, somewhere in the corridors, *Dada* (another friend who is also named as Atul) screamed,

"*Girish, Mahatria ki Unposted Letters book kharid lenaa.*" [Buy the book 'Unposted Letters', authored by Mahatria.]

In the middle of the crowd moving out from the auditorium, I managed to reach the book counter and bought that book called by *Dada*. It remained on my bookshelf for several months. Later, I picked it and took out time to read. My first read was casual, and my thoughts were driven intellectually appreciating the content as good stuff for the purpose of writing a book but difficult to implement in day-to-day living by any person with a family life.

In my close circle of friends, which is named as '*masti ki paathshaalaa*', they wanted me to take up a review of a book. I chose this book and created a Power Point presentation for my delivery in the group. I gave my presentation, which happened almost a year after the book was bought. In this second read of the book for the purpose of making the presentation, I could synch in its content and relate it to my life situations. This time, the vibes were different, definitely they were not purely intellectual but something more than that. Still, the spiritual spark was missing.

Then the incident of November 2014 took place. Fast forward, fast forward, in June 2015, I received a call from the Indore Management Association (IMA) to do a review of this book for its members. I was overwhelmed to note how they knew that I would be doing it with utmost joy and willingness, as so much within me had undergone transformation by this time. During the third read of this book to prepare for my session for IMA, my eyes were flooded with positive tears, making me understand the depth and truth of its content, that is, the teachings of my Master. I could deliver the session successfully before the IMA members by His grace and by feeling His presence.

I got 'that connection' while giving all these reviews.

Since I had been socially active, I was fortunate to clear the selection interview to become a member of the *Leo Club of Indore Main,* where admission happened only with the unanimous consent of its entire governing board. This Club is one of the most elite and oldest active social clubs in the entire global fraternity of Lions' International, USA.

This club gave me the perfect ecosystem to bring out my creativity, gave me the freedom to implement innovative ideas, and allowed me to put forth new perspectives and dimensions to what already existed. There were several *'for the first time'* activities and initiatives that unfolded during my close to ten-year tenure in this club. And this is a common experience for every member of this prestigious club. I could scale up to the responsible role of president of this club, with my initial journey starting with the editorship of its monthly magazine. Sumit during his tenure of presidentship gave me the opportunity to be the editor of the prestigious monthly magazine which prior to me taking the charge had never been printed but was photocopied. For the first time in its history, it got printed despite strict budgetary constraints given by the president. Later, I had also held the post of Honorary Secretary.

An informal offshoot of this formal club was created with the name *Leo Legends* which is an integral part of my life, as if an extended family. This is a group that is made of highly successful and abundance-minded people who enjoy their own as well as others' success, keeping their own peace intact. All these wonderful souls befit the essence of the oxymorons of being 'peacefully successful' and 'ambitiously satisfied'. The bonding, love, affection, and warmth shared among all of its members is beyond comprehension. It's a world akin to what my Master has created and is striving to expand it through His teachings. In giving the world, creative events for it to experience, I got a whole world of so many beautiful, loving souls.

Among all these social setups, there is a concentric circle of family-knitted friends, a set of nine couples along with their children, called *'Challengers'*. Its foundation was laid on my maiden trip in the winter of 2010 when four couples out of the present nine visited the National Tiger Reserve Park of Kanha-Kisli. In order to make our vocabulary positive, we were talking about avoiding negative words. Among several words, the word 'problem' came up many times, and we learned to use the word *'challenge'*, instead. This word hit everyone so much during the entire trip that each one started calling the other a *'challenger'*. The thirteen years since its inception have led to scores of joyful and happy moments in the lives of entire groups, including children. In reciprocation, we all have a *'family of families.'*

In January 2012, a bunch of 20 crazy adventurists, including renowned personalities of the city, went for the Mumbai marathon which required running of 42 kilometers. Based on their experience, they felt the need to bring this kind of an event to Indore instead of everyone traveling to Mumbai every year. Work started to make this feeling a reality, and I was also taken in for its brainstorming since I had been an active sportsperson and had common connections. Together, we founded a charitable body, the Academy of Indore Marathoners (AIM), to organize running events in Indore and around. The larger-than-life objective for this body had been to bring the entire city into a health and fitness regime. We, as part of its core team worked relentlessly to bring awareness about this aspect of life.

In January 2013, I participated in the Mumbai event for my maiden half marathon. This year, we all came together with more zeal and a clear strategy for organizing the magnanimous running event at Indore which could eventually materialize in February 2015 after relentless efforts by the entire core team. The sponsors and media came together, the local administration and traffic police supported us wholeheartedly, and we at AIM could do it. Though I was physically not present at the event, being bedridden, I cherish the preparatory journey for the same wherein I was intensely involved. It was the participation of several thousand people in a professionally organized running event at Indore that altered the health and fitness contours of the entire city. There was so much giving and getting, a truly phenomenal experience. We at AIM could also conceptualize the first-ever monsoon night half marathon event named as *'Rainathon'*, which has become a signature event of the city. The name signifies *'rain'* for the monsoon season and *'raina'* which in Hindi language signifies night.

In giving myself selflessly to this venture of AIM, I was bestowed with the responsibility of taking up the role of Honorary Secretary for two years. I also got connected to several truly inspiring souls who are *'look up to'* personalities for me in their respective domains, be it fitness, disciplined execution, business processes, branding, planning, and strategy. Sudarshan and I connected to pursue long-distance cycling on Sundays and explored several beautiful, serene spots in the range of 50 to 60 kilometers around Indore. We would pedal more and talk less, and in those silent zones between us, we carried the assurance of each other. An unspoken understanding was created. We could communicate between us at the thought level. We developed unity and became a creative team together.

In the entire journey of my professional career so far, I got the chance to be with several team members and worked for several clients and professionals. The synergy with everyone had been impeccable. In my pursuits, each one helped each other. For my seniors, I would make efforts to push them up the ladder of career progression, which in turn made that place available for me to progress. I adopted a synergistic process, and it worked well, a win-win for all the stakeholders. When opinions were sought from me in my role, I would provide alternatives with an objective analysis as well as my own recommendations. My solution-centric approach made the senior management take decisions with ease, and within a short period of time, I could become part of that senior management group. All this expanded my horizons, and I could grow and evolve immensely.

While servicing the clients during the tenure of my professional practice, creating a delight by going the extra mile and advising or developing a process flow that created efficiency in their business operations was the winning model for my service deliveries. Taking help from fellow professionals and venturing out for untouched areas of work with the intent of helping the client was yet another approach that brought humongous sustainable success all around. This led me to get associated with several excellent professional experts across the country, building long-lasting client relationships.

My Master visited Indore on February 18th, 2023, after almost ten years since 2013. I have already mentioned when my first experience happened with my Master. This time for His second visit, I gave everything I could to make His visit as meaningful as possible for the larger benefit of the city as a whole. I had no expectations, no wanting, no desires; I just wanted to be there and contribute in all the possible ways for a seamless experience for everyone who would be part of the program. In return, I gained the most, unexpectedly and incomprehensibly. Akshat received spiritual attention from my Master for the pursuit of his passion. For me, it was an experience of history repeating itself: *Sri Sathya Sai Baba* coming and pouring divinity into me, and now, my Master blessing Akshat.

There has never been any sense of insecurity within me. Sports had given me a strong sense of personal security, for which I knew, the source was within. This intrinsic security within me resulted in abundant success in several dimensions of life. It was reflected multi-dimensionally.

All of this came from giving, contributing, being in a creative zone, helping others in their pursuits, being with them in a meaningful way, and influencing their motives without any need for my recognition. With all these synergies, abundance flowed in. I was getting everything.

Giving is an expression of gratitude, joy, and trust. In other words, it is doing God's work. Despite having no expectation of having a return favor, God does everything to fulfill one's desires. For me, the attribute of giving brought God into my team. And once HE became a part of my team, how could I not win in life?

Let this life be filled and fulfilled with *giving and getting...*

तू लुटाता रहा, मैं पाता रहा।
तू खुशियों का खजाना भरता रहा।

बगैर मांगे सब कुछ दिया,
इतना दिया कि मैं वापस देता रहूं तो भी ख़त्म न हो

10

Life of This and That Sides...

Owing to a variety of experiences and exposures, many a times I had been posed with one common question: *"How do you feel being on this side now?"*

The reference to 'side' had been in the context of where I stood or what I achieved at that point in time.

It also relates to the *'inside'* and the *'outside'*, to which I kept referring in my expressions.

In recent times, my reply to the above question has been,

"There are no sides; for me, it's a 360° perspective of the same whole, a complete experience in itself. And when we draw a 360° view, it comes out as a 'circle'. A circle doesn't have sides. There is no start or an end to it. It's a continuum..."

Each exposure or experience is unique to itself. One need not be compared with the other. Truly, they are incomparable since elements of learning or maturity creeps in by going through them.

It's just one whole thing. How can a wave be different from the ocean or you and me from life? One is the reflection of the other. Everything is just the same, just one, without any sides.

My Master says, "*How far is the mud-pot from the mud and the gold-necklace from the gold?*"

The form is created by the formless. I arrived in this manifested world in an embodied form, and that formless carried me through from there to here and is now carrying me from here to there. I was born as a child to be parented by my parents. Arpita and I are blessed to have Akshat through us, and he is being parented by us.

Life filled me with several enlightened teachers who imparted teachings to shape me up. I was fortunate enough that I could offer myself as a coach to the school football team immediately after passing out my Class XII and devote my time and energy with the team during the 'after school extended sports period' and on weekends to coach them, and assist the sports teacher. I was taught, and I could teach.

As the House Captain of *Narmada* House, in the school morning assembly, I would read newspaper headlines during the turn of our house. There were occasions, by the grace of God, when I was part of the newspaper headlines, winning accolades, or, on certain other occasions, I drafted press notes for news coverage of the events for which I was part of the organizing teams, be it blood donation camps, plantation drives, marathons, tournaments, and so on.

Being part of the first batch of the school, I would be looked up to as a senior all throughout. Later in my career progression, I was fortunate to have several super-fine individuals whom I could look up to. I continue to have such wonderful 'look-up to' personalities, even in the present.

While studying for CA, I attended coaching classes to get the benefit of expert knowledge and skills from the best-in-class subject experts. After achieving the CA qualification, I was honored to get an opportunity to teach and coach the subject of cost accounting to the students of the CA final stage in one of the renowned CA coaching institutes in the city, which I did for close to 6 years apart from pursuing the profession. Within the period of these 6 years, with the assistance of Navin, lovingly called as *Nanu*, both of us together had set up our own classes in his CA office for which I would go early morning to his home to take the keys of the office, open it, set up the class room and give my lecture. Thereafter, I would go to my work place by returning the key to him.

There are several medals, trophies, and cups that find their way into the showcase at my home and office. At the same time, there are several events conceptualized and organized in which I could contribute my bit, whereby the potential of several worthy individuals surfaced, and they were recognized with similar medals, trophies, and cups.

In my professional pursuit, I had been an auditor, making all the efforts to give value-added services, and at the same time, I got to play the role of an auditee while working for a corporation, ensuring to implement the guidance and consultation received for optimizing the performance.

In the courtroom while practicing income-tax litigation, I was on the side of the taxpayer, assisting the bench to arrive at the appropriate decision on the issue involved. Now, I sit in the chair on this side, to hear the arguments from the litigating parties, to arrive at the decision.

For me, it has always been a regular feature to attend several knowledge-sharing events, such as study circle meetings, seminars, or conferences, to understand the nuances of the various domains I plunged into. Later, life gave me many occasions to exchange my learnings and experiences gained from walking the path I treaded. For me, it has been both, extending the mementos and floral welcomes to the guest speakers as well as receiving the same as a guest speaker from the organizers. All this has humbled me.

I learned to write. Presently, I am writing to learn.

It has always been a celebration for me, being in such *'circles'* of 360°.

We all cross each other through the realm of our personalities, by which we are shaped. There is a need to know who the others are, their roles, and their structures. Involvements and engagement lead to the building of several relationships. Some relations are momentary, some are specific to the activity, some relationships continue for the distance to fade away gradually, and some remain for a lifetime.

Relationships are the vehicles through which we meet and interact. Too much attachment to the relationship turns it into possessiveness, breaking the *flow of the circle* into this side and that side, making it linear. A split is created because of attachment, which is anti-nature.

Making each one grow by giving the desired space and an approach of *'you help me and I help you'* shifts the linear tendency to re-mold it into a circular flow. Let there be no wanting, no expectations; just keep doing and flowing with the flow to take care of everything.

You want...

You want to possess, he slips away

You want to control, to lose him on the way

You want to impose, for him to disobey

You want to question, no answers coming your way

You want to doubt, giving him a fearful bout

You want to complain, but love is his domain

You want to rant, for which nothing he will grant

You only want to speak, he becoming nothing but weak

You want pampers, he is tired of giving hampers

You shun the responsibility, questioning his ability

You want him to live your way, only space will bring all the joy and cheerful gay.

On one occasion, I was fortunate enough to get valuable learnings and realizations during a stargazing session, which was conducted by an expert for a group of children in a social club called Young Indians (YI) of which I was a member. Akshat was part of that group of children, and I stood along with him out of curiosity to learn about stargazing. The person was explaining to children about the sky around us and said,

"Every celestial body in the Universe is in a state of motion for it to exist, lest it explode and vanish."

This reality statement by him resonated within me with the science of *'karm yog'* as explained by Lord *Krishn* and enunciated in the epic *'Bhagwat Geeta'* and echoed in my mind at that very moment that we are all part of the Universe and need to be in a *state of motion* for our existence.

Life is action; it is all about application. The five elements that constitute life, namely, earth, water, fire, air, and space, all reflect this attribute of action.

Earth is always rotating and revolving in its orbit, a 360° movement. It is moving from there to here and here to there continuously, with seasons changing on their own, which otherwise would not occur.

Water flows freely on its own, seeking its own level. It changes forms to become vapor, steam, snow, or ice and regains its originality. There are cyclical high and low tides that keep it in motion. Stagnant water is a breeding ground for pathogens and creates health issues.

Fire always flares upward. The flames are always dancing and maneuvering, exuberating energy and enthusiasm. They are flexible and spread warmth when a safe distance is kept; otherwise, they may cause damage.

Air is always flowing and churning itself. There is speed, motion in it. It acts as a carrier of oxygen, fragrance, clouds, pollens and seeds, adding life to life. In its stillness, one feels suffocation. Air in a closed room smells foul.

Space is always expanding so that it can embrace everything. By expanding, it allows everyone an equal opportunity, giving everyone the required space to open up and express themselves. When it is curtailed, there can't be any blossoming.

Holistically, it is an overwhelming feeling. Let this 360° circle keep rotating, keep flowing with energy and enthusiasm, keep expanding its circumference, and encompass as much as it can during this one lifetime, whatever the side. Let it all be out of devotion, sincerity, and happiness.

II

Flowing like a River, Mantra of My Life…

They always say, work hard to succeed
And I wonder how hard river worked to ultimately achieve the end

The world is mean, for the end you dared to achieve
I had to go n bow down taking bends here and there

The icy rock in me had to melt first, for my first achievement to attain the flow

The start is so unnoticeable, but transformative springboard to my future

For I am shallow and noisy,
They come for the picnic and take a ride with me, like a roller coaster
I rumble without a grumble in the rapids
Ripping apart the ripples within

I don't have the banks on my sides
In my rage, I move the mountains, making them rounded pebbles,
To see those as my medals

With pride, as a misnomer, I attain the height
But only to encounter the cliff for the fall

Deep within, I am eternally optimistic and creative
To fly down arrogantly, for they to see a scenic waterfall

They come down for a picture and jacuzzi massage,
For a feel to be on the high
I know what it is to take a hit on the rocks
And make my way to bring visibility to the world

The fall leads me to higher maturities
Removing all the ambiguities
I am now serene and compassionate
Because
Throughout the path, I am so sincere n passionate

Giving and serving everything, now on the way
Flowing deep in calmness, now with abundant banks
The stillness and silence are now part of my glow
They get astonished seeing me flowing with the flow

Serving Thy purpose is the goal
Me realizing, they found me useful
I am now arriving, is a feeling so beautiful

He is embracing and taking me in
I find, there is no me and He, as it all became, WE at the seashore

It will start over again, with the scorching heat of the Sun,
Part of WE will disappear in vapors
Some drop on the way and others flake away

The snow hardens as it reaches mountain-high
Remember,
To succeed and achieve that flow, melt it must

Once in a flow, I am bound to grow…

www.ingramcontent.com/pod-product-compliance
Lightning Source LLC
Chambersburg PA
CBHW061343160726
47995CB00001B/153